Better Homes and Gardens®

CHRISTMAS

FROM THE HEART®

Volume 16

Meredith® Books
Des Moines, Iowa

Better Homes and Gardens®
CHRISTMAS
FROM THE HEART®

Editor: Jessica Saari
Contributing Editor: Carol Field Dahlstrom
Contributing Food Editor: Winifred Moranville
Associate Design Director: Todd Emerson Hanson
Contributing Designer: Angie Haupert Hoogensen
Copy Chief: Terri Fredrickson
Copy Editor: Kevin Cox
Publishing Operations Manager: Karen Schirm
Senior Editor, Asset and Information Manager: Phillip Morgan
Edit and Design Production Coordinator: Mary Lee Gavin
Editorial Assistant: Cheryl Eckert
Book Production Managers: Pam Kvitne, Marjorie
   J. Schenkelberg, Rick von Holdt, Mark Weaver
Contributing Copy Editor: Sarah Oliver Watson
Contributing Proofreaders: Judy Friedman, Karen Grossman,
   Jody Speer
Contributing Photographers: Pete Krumhardt, Scott Little,
   Dean Tanner/Primary Image, Jay Wilde
Contributing Technical Illustrator: Chris Neubauer
   Graphics, Inc.
Contributing Project Designers: Kristin Detrick, Marilyn Losee,
   Janet Petersma, Margaret Sindelar, Jan Temeyer
Contributing Recipe Development: Carrie Holcomb
Contributing Photostyling Assistant: Donna Chesnut
Test Kitchen Director: Lynn Blanchard
Test Kitchen Product Supervisor: Jill Moberly

Meredith® Books
Executive Director, Editorial: Gregory H. Kayko
Executive Director, Design: Matt Strelecki
Managing Editor: Amy Tincher-Durik
Executive Editor: Jennifer Darling
Senior Editor/Group Manager: Jan Miller
Senior Associate Design Director: Ken Carlson

Publisher and Editor in Chief: James D. Blume
Editorial Director: Linda Raglan Cunningham
Executive Director, New Business Development: Todd M. Davis
Executive Director, Sales: Ken Zagor
Director, Operations: George A. Susral
Director, Production: Douglas M. Johnston
Director, Marketing & Publicity: Amy Nichols
Business Director: Jim Leonard

Vice President and General Manager: Douglas J. Guendel

Better Homes and Gardens® Magazine
Editor in Chief: Gayle Goodson Butler
Deputy Editor, Home Design: Oma Blaise Ford
Deputy Editor, Food and Entertaining: Nancy Wall Hopkins

Meredith Publishing Group
President: Jack Griffin
Senior Vice President: Karla Jeffries
Vice President, Corporate Solutions: Michael Brownstein
Vice President, Creative Services: Ellen de Lathouder
Vice President, Manufacturing: Bruce Heston
Vice President, Consumer Marketing: David Ball
Consumer Product Associate Marketing Director: Steve Swanson
Consumer Product Marketing Manager: Wendy Merical
Business Manager: Darren Tollefson

Meredith Corporation
Chairman of the Board: William T. Kerr
President and Chief Executive Officer: Steve Lacy

In Memoriam: E.T. Meredith III (1933-2003)

All of us at Meredith® Books are dedicated to providing you
with information and ideas to enhance your home. We welcome
your comments and suggestions. Write to us at: Meredith Books
Editorial Department, 1716 Locust St., Des Moines, IA
50309-3023. *Christmas from the Heart 2007* is available by mail.
To order editions from past years, call 800/627-5490.

Our seal assures you that every recipe in
Christmas from the Heart 2007 has been tested
in the Better Homes and Gardens® Test Kitchen.
This means that each recipe is practical and
reliable, and meets our high standards of taste
appeal. We guarantee your satisfaction with
this book for as long as you own it.

Better Homes and Gardens®

CHRISTMAS

FROM THE HEART®

contents

Complement your traditional Christmas red with some pretty apple green this season. Create sparkling ornaments like these **Glitter and Bead Ornaments** and **Berry Trims,** *above.* Round candles in a row become a stunning centerpiece. The **Scallop-Trimmed Candles,** *opposite,* are made using dried leaves and flower heads. Instructions for all of the projects are on *page 16.*

tradition
with a twist

You love to decorate for the holidays in traditional style, but this year change it up a bit with new colors and textures to give an unexpected yet traditional twist.

Purchased ornaments that are broken (or become broken) take on a new life as pieces of painted mosaic in these **Sparkling Mosaic Ornaments,** *opposite*. Naturally dried flowers and leaves purchased at a crafts store layer nicely on a square wreath to make a **Squared Holiday Wreath,** *above*. A big red traditional bow finishes the wreath for hanging. Instructions are on *pages 17–18.*

Beautifully traditional toile is available in Christmas print fabric during the holiday season. Choose these prints to make our **Poinsettia-Embroidered Stocking,** *opposite,* and **Poinsettia-Topped Pillow,** *below.* The stocking has a coordinating cotton print cuff with ivory embroidery and features a piping trim. A 3-D poinsettia made from suede finishes the pillow. Instructions are on *pages 18–21.*

Fill a tree with some beautiful ornaments that you make yourself. Use your favorite ribbon to make **Pretty Pleated Pinwheels,** *opposite,* to showcase your colors of the season. Complete the tree with purchased ornaments that complement your ribbon choice. Top off your holiday decorating with a **Red-Topped Trio,** *below,* featuring traditional red ornaments. Each ornament is trimmed with just one embellishment. Instructions for all of the projects are on *page 22.*

For a last-minute holiday statement, create a **Simple Bowed Pillow,** *above,* by tying a festive lime green ribbon and beaded tassel around a purchased pillow. Choose a flat-front picture frame and embellish it with traditional holiday berries and ribbon. Then fill the frame with a pretty scrapbook paper to make a **Paper-Filled Frame,** *opposite.* Instructions for both projects are on *page 23.*

Glitter and Bead Ornaments

Shown on page 6

WHAT YOU NEED

Purchased apple green matte-finish
    ornaments
Tumbler
Crafts glue
Red bugle beads
Fine green glitter
24-gauge red wire
Green beads to fit on the wire

HERE'S HOW

Place an ornament in the tumbler to
secure it while working. Use crafts glue to
make lines from the top of the ornament
to about one-third of the way down the
ornament. Add a bugle bead at the end
of each glue line. Sprinkle with glitter.
Add more glue around the ornament top
and allow to dry. Thread the green beads
on the wire, bending the end of the wire
to keep the beads from falling off.
Position the beads on the wire and add a
dot of glue on both sides to secure. Let
the glue dry. Twist the wire and add to
the top of the ornament for a hanger.

Berry Trims

Shown on cover and page 6

WHAT YOU NEED

Wire
Purchased berry sprigs
Purchased fabric leaves
Sheer fabric ribbon

HERE'S HOW

Wire the leaves to the berry sprigs.
Tie a bow at the top of the grouping of
berries and leaves. Add a wire hanger
for hanging.

Scallop-Trimmed Candles

Shown on page 7

WHAT YOU NEED

Strand of polished green stones
3 round green candles; straight pins
Wire cutters; scissors
Red eucalyptus petals
Green eucalyptus petals
Hot glue gun and glue sticks
Small dried red flowers

HERE'S HOW

1. Cut the strand of stones and secure one
end of the strand with tape. (You may need
to remove some stones to reveal enough
string to secure.) Create three smaller
strands of green stones to top each
candle. The strand of stones should rest
approximately ½ inch down from the top
edge of the candle away from the flame.
Remove stones as needed to expose some
string at each end of the strand. Knot each
strand tightly and cut off excess string.
Lay each strand of stones on a candle top.
2. Snip several straight pins by
approximately ¼ inch. Layer a red and
green eucalyptus petal. Using a straight
pin, pierce the top of each petal and push
into a candle just below the strand of
stones (touching the stones). Apply hot
glue to the top edges of the petals,
immersing the bottom of the stones as
well. Press one dried flower into the hot
glue. (This will help secure the strand of
stones and hide the hot glue.) Repeat this
procedure all the way around each candle.

Never leave a burning candle unattended.

Sparkling Mosaic Ornaments
Shown on page 8

WHAT YOU NEED
Protective gloves and eye wear
Purchased red ornaments
Decorative ornaments (the same size
    and shape as the red ornaments)
Large resealable bag
Small hammer
Tray
Pencil
Wood cuticle stick
Gold dimensional texture paint
Fine gold glitter

HERE'S HOW
1. Put on protective gloves and eyewear.
Remove hanger top from decorative
ornaments. Place one decorative
ornament in a resealable bag and seal it
(Photo A). On a protected surface break
ornament into pieces by tapping with a
hammer (Photo B). Pour ornament pieces
into a tray or container with low sides.
Break additional decorative ornaments
as needed to obtain desired shapes.
2. Place an ornament piece onto the
surface of a red ornament. Trace around
the piece with a pencil (Photo C). Using
a wood cuticle stick, apply the texture
paint to the red ornament in and around
the pencil outline (Photo D). Press the
ornament piece into the texture paint,
ensuring that all sharp edges are
submerged in the texture medium (Photo
E). Immediately sprinkle the area with
fine gold glitter. Hang ornament to dry.

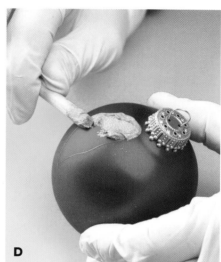

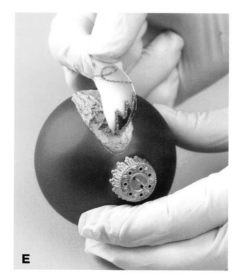

Squared Holiday Wreath
Shown on page 9

WHAT YOU NEED
Plastic foam square frame
    14×14 inches such as Styrofoam
Red acrylic paint
Foam brush
Dried red ball mums
Hot glue gun and glue sticks
Dried red protea flowers
Red Christmas potpourri
Dried red roses
Red beaded garland
Scissors
Red ribbon bow

HERE'S HOW
1. On a protected surface paint plastic foam frame red using foam brush. Let dry. Arrange three ball mums in one corner of the frame. Reduce mum sizes (if desired) by removing some outside petals. Hot-glue mums in place. Add protea flowers on each side of the mums. Hot-glue in place. Cover the remaining front frame area with red potpourri petals.
2. Add dried red roses around the frame for accent. Swirl red beaded garland around the top surface of the frame and hot-glue in place. Add a printed red ribbon bow to the corner of the wreath using hot glue.

Poinsettia-Topped Pillow
Shown on page 10

WHAT YOU NEED
14 inch pillow form
½ yard red toile Christmas print cotton
    fabric
½ yard red cotton print fabric
⅛ yard red checked cotton fabric for
    cording
2 yards of ¼-inch-wide cotton cording
Tracing paper or copier
⅛ yard red suede fabric
Scrap of two-sided fusible webbing
Three ⅜-inch round shank buttons
Brown fine-line permanent fabric pen
Matching thread; scissors

HERE'S HOW
Cut toile print fabric into squares as defined by the print, and piece together with red cotton fabric to make a 15½-inch square. This project started with an 8½-inch center and 4-inch corner squares. Cut a 15½-inch square from toile fabric for pillow back. Cut checked fabric into 1½-inch-wide strips to cover cording. Baste close to cording, using a zipper foot. Baste piping to outside edges of pillow front. Clip and trim corners. With right sides together, stitch pillow front to back, stitching just inside basting line for piping, leaving an opening 6-8 inches wide to insert pillow form. Insert pillow form and stitch opening closed.

To make poinsettia decoration:
Using press cloth, iron fusible webbing onto back of piece of suede fabric. Remove paper backing and fuse another piece of suede fabric onto first piece. Copy three poinsettia patterns and cut pieces from double thickness of suede fabric. Using the permanent fabric marker, draw center leaf veins onto each flower petal. Using needle and matching thread, take a couple of larger stitches in the center of the largest flower piece and gather up center slightly to curl petals. Add middle-size piece to top and stitch through both layers to join, taking a couple of stitches through only the center layer to gather up flower a bit. Add smallest flower shape to top, stitching through all three layers and gathering up top petals to curl slightly. Stitch to corner of center square of pillow. Sew three small buttons to center of poinsettia.

POINSETTIA-TOPPED PILLOW
Full-Size Patterns

Poinsettia-Embroidered Stocking

Shown on page 11

WHAT YOU NEED
Tracing paper; scissors
⅓ yard cotton poinsettia print fabric
⅓ yard cotton print fabric for lining and cuff
⅛ yard plaid fabric for piping
Scraps checked fabric for toe/heel of stocking
Scraps of two-sided fusible webbing
1⅛ yard of ¼ inch cording
Three ⅜-inch round shank buttons
Red and ecru embroidery floss; needle
Matching thread
Light-colored carbon paper

HERE'S HOW
1. Enlarge the patterns, *opposite*, onto tracing paper and cut out. With right sides together, cut two of the stocking patterns from each of the poinsettia and cotton lining fabrics. From print fabric, cut a 2×7-inch strip for the hanging loop and two pieces from cuff pattern. Cut heel and toe pieces from checked fabric. From plaid fabric cut 1-inch wide strips of fabric for the piping around stocking.

2. Trace heel and toe pieces onto paper backing of fusible webbing. Fuse webbing to back of plaid fabric and cut out shapes. Fuse onto front of poinsettia stocking piece and work the blanket stitch around the edges using two to three strands of red floss. (See stitching diagrams, *page 160*.) To make piping, wrap a 1-inch-wide strip of fabric around cording and baste close to cording using a zipper foot. Baste piping around edge of stocking front side and lower edges. With right sides together stitch around side edges of the stocking and lining pieces, leaving top edges open using a ¼-inch seam allowance. Clip curves and turn stocking pieces right side out. Insert lining inside stocking, with wrong sides together and top edges even.

3. With right sides together, sew long edge of loop piece together. Turn right side out. Transfer poinsettia flower pattern, *below*, to center of one cuff piece of fabric, tracing lines of pattern over light-colored carbon paper. Embroider the stem stitch along design lines, using 2 strands of ecru floss. (See stitching diagrams, *page 160*.) With right sides together, sew short side of cuff piece to form a circular tube. Turn right side out and fold in half, pressing lightly. Place

**POINSETTIA-
EMBROIDERED
STOCKING**
Full-Size Pattern

hanging loop down inside stocking at side edge; overlap raw edges of ends at top edge of stocking. Baste through all layers of stocking, lining, and loop. Insert cuff inside stocking, with right side of cuff against the right side of the stocking lining, keeping top raw edges even. Sew around top edge through all layers, using a ⅜-inch seam allowance.

4. Flip cuff piece out over front of stocking. Sew buttons to center of poinsettia stitching.

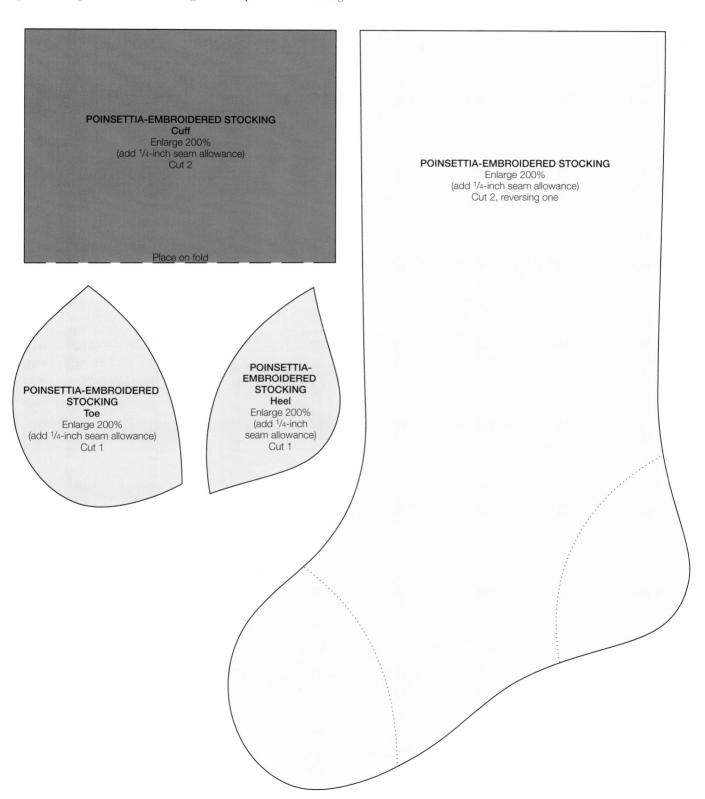

POINSETTIA-EMBROIDERED STOCKING
Cuff
Enlarge 200%
(add ¼-inch seam allowance)
Cut 2

Place on fold

POINSETTIA-EMBROIDERED STOCKING
Enlarge 200%
(add ¼-inch seam allowance)
Cut 2, reversing one

POINSETTIA-EMBROIDERED STOCKING
Toe
Enlarge 200%
(add ¼-inch seam allowance)
Cut 1

POINSETTIA-EMBROIDERED STOCKING
Heel
Enlarge 200%
(add ¼-inch seam allowance)
Cut 1

Pretty Pleated Pinwheels
Shown on page 13

WHAT YOU NEED
Compass
8×12-inch piece of cardboard
Scissors
2 yards 3-inch-wide satin ribbon in
    desired color
Crafts glue suitable for gluing fabric
Saucer
18 inches of cording with flat stitching
    on one side

HERE'S HOW
1. Using the compass, draw a 5-inch
circle and a 2-inch circle onto cardboard.
Cut out. Set the 2-inch circle aside.
Draw a 1-inch circle in the center of
the 5-inch circle. Pleating the ribbon as
you go, glue the folded ribbon following
the lines of the drawn circle, slightly
overlapping the lines to the inside.
2. Continue gluing the pleated ribbon
onto the large cardboard circle until the
circle is complete. Cut off any excess
ribbon. Set a saucer on top of the ribbon
to weight it down as it dries. Cut a 3-inch
circle from the ribbon. Set the 2-inch
cardboard circle in the center of the back
side of the ribbon circle. Glue the edges
to the back. Glue the cording behind the
circle, trimming any excess cording.
Remove the saucer and glue the small
circle in the center of the larger circle.
Allow to dry.

Red-Topped Trio
Shown on page 12

WHAT YOU NEED
Red satin-finish ball ornaments
Red fur-like material
Scissors
Double-sided tape
⅜-inch-wide red sheer ribbon trim with
    red acrylic beads
Strong crafts glue such as Quick Grip
    all-purpose permanent adhesive
Red miniature garland

HERE'S HOW
to make the Fur-Topped Ornament
Cut one piece of fur in the shape of
a circle with a three-inch diameter.
Measure the opening on a plastic
container or use a compass and piece
of paper. Cut a slit to the center of the
circle. Cut out a small circular hole for
the top of the ornament. Trim the circle
until it lies flat on the ornament.
Adhere the material to the ornament
using double-sided tape.

HERE'S HOW
to make the Beaded Ribbon Ornament
Wrap beaded ribbon trim around the
center of an ornament. Secure the ribbon
to the ornament using double-sided tape
trimming tape if necessary. If needed, use
crafts glue to secure.

HERE'S HOW
**to make the Garland-Topped
Ornament**
Carefully glue one end of the garland
to the top of the ornament. Let dry.
Begin wrapping garland around
ornament, gluing the bottom of garland
to ornament. Use crafts glue sparingly.
Snip off excess garland. Allow to dry.

Simple Bowed Pillow
Shown on page 14

WHAT YOU NEED
Purchased pillow in red or green
3 yards 2-inch-wide double-faced satin
    ribbon in opposite color
Scissors
Purchased beaded tassel
Narrow ribbon (optional)

HERE'S HOW
Lay the pillow on a flat surface and
crisscross the ribbon as if wrapping a
package. Attach the tassel at the bow
using the loop on the tassel or with
narrow ribbon.

Paper-Filled Frame
Shown on cover and page 15

WHAT YOU NEED:
Purchased wood frame
3 red berries with leaves floral picks
Christmas card stock sticker (long
    and thin)
Christmas scrapbook paper
    (primarily green)
Heart embellishment (optional)
Thin green ribbon
Clear tiny marbles
Hot glue gun and glue sticks
Double-sided tape
Wire snips
Small cup
Box

HERE'S HOW
1. Lay frame flat and line up the
placement of long scrapbook sticker.
Apply sticker and wrap around sides of
frame to the back. Cut off excess. Pour
clear marbles in a small cup. Apply
double-sided tape to surface of sticker
(front and sides) in long horizontal strips.

If double-sided tape is thinner than
sticker width, apply tape to top edge of
sticker (without removing the paper
backing), then apply tape to bottom edge
of sticker. Remove backing from top and
bottom strips then add a middle strip of
tape overlapping the others. Remove
paper backing and hold taped area over
a box. Gently pour clear marbles over
sections of the taped sticker. Gently press
the marbles into place. Shake off excess
and repeat this procedure until all of the
tape is covered.
2. Using wire snips, cut off excess length
on berry picks. Lay out placement of
picks and hot-glue in place. If adding
heart embellishment (shown on cover),
tape a thin piece of ribbon to the back
of the heart embellishment. Hot-glue
ribbon to front of frame. Insert a favorite
scrapbooking paper, holiday card,
or photograph in the frame.

baby's
first
christmas

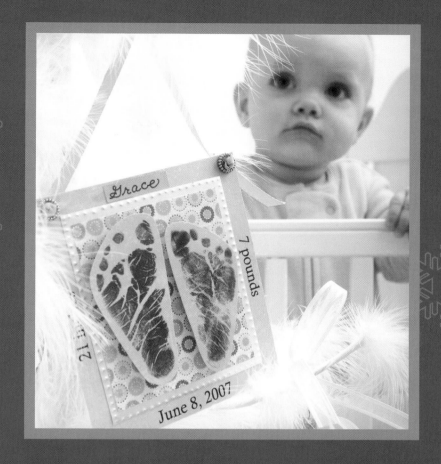

Grace

7 pounds

June 8, 2007

What could be more beautiful than to celebrate Christmas with all the things that remind you of your new baby?

Fill the tree with the little one in mind by creating **Sweet Baby Shoe Ornaments,** *opposite,* from purchased baby shoes and bits of tiny flowers. To make a keepsake ornament especially for baby, use a tiny footprint to mark the special occasion with a **Baby Footprint Ornament,** *above.* Instructions for both projects are on *page 34.*

In pastel colors so soothing and sweet, create **Soft Polka-Dot Stockings,** *opposite,* from fleece. The stockings are just the right size to hang for that first Christmas. Trim the cuff with the name or monogram of the special baby by using hand or machine stitches, monograms, or couched ribbon. Instructions and patterns to make the stockings are on *pages 35–36.*

Make some ornaments that are sure to keep your little one happy.

Fill the **Treat Cones,** *above,* with breakfast cereal or other safe treats

to hang on the tree. Purchased blankets can become beautifully

personalized with just a bit of sewing from you. Create the **Blanket**

Trims, *opposite,* by adding your own special stitches and trims.

Instructions are on *pages 36–37.*

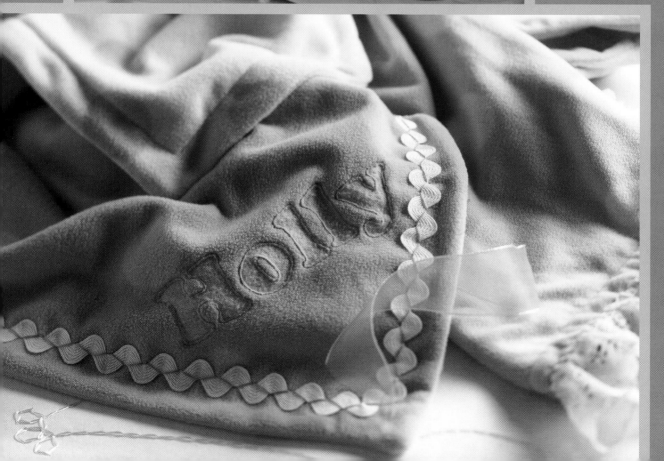

Create a **Message Cone Tree,** *above,* that conveys hopes and
dreams for the little one. Created from colorful scrapbook papers
and message charms, the tree can say whatever you wish. Sure to
become an heirloom, baby's **Love Quilt,** *opposite,* is certainly made
from the heart. Pieced using tiny printed fabrics, this sweet coverlet
will be a favorite. Instructions and patterns are on *pages 38–41.*

Create a unique display on your mantel by using baby bottles for an unexpected decoration. **Sugar Bottles,** *opposite,* are filled with colored decorator sugars, tied with a ribbon bow, and arranged on the mantel. Instructions are on *page 41.*

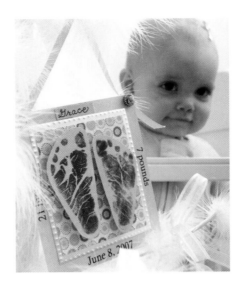

Sweet Baby Shoe Ornaments
Shown on page 24

WHAT YOU NEED
Purchased baby shoes in desired color
  and style, preferably with a strap
Tiny satin flowers on stems (available at
  crafts stores)
Crafts glue or hot glue and glue gun
¼-wide satin ribbon in matching color

HERE'S HOW
Take out any labels in the shoe. Glue or
wrap the stems of the roses around the
strap of the shoe. Tie a bow with the
ribbon. Glue onto the strap. Tie on tree
with another piece of matching ribbon.

Baby Footprint Ornament
Shown on page 25

WHAT YOU NEED
Baby's footprints
Two pieces of light-colored scrapbook
  paper
Silver card stock with satin finish
Paper glaze such as Aleene's Paper
  Glaze
Paintbrush; scissors
Embossing stylist tool
Two-sided adhesive foam dots
Double-sided tape
Crafts knife
Access to computer/printer/copier or
  letter stickers
⅜-inch-wide ribbon
2 silver rondelle beads

HERE'S HOW
1. Copy an image of baby's footprints
onto a piece of light-colored scrapbook
paper. Brush two coats of paper glaze onto
the scrapbook paper, allowing drying time
in between. (This will protect the paper
from fingerprints and dust, etc.)
2. Cut out the paper footprints. Cut a
square of colored scrapbook paper large
enough to display the footprints. Cut a
slightly larger square of silver card stock.
Turn silver paper over and lay it on a soft
surface such as a piece of craft foam or
cardboard. Using a stylist tool make dot
impressions around the edge of the square.
3. Apply foam dots (two layers) to the
back of footprints. Apply footprints to
square of colored scrapbook paper.
Apply paper square to square of silver
paper using double-sided tape.
4. The next step can be done two ways:
Option 1: Cut out a square of scrapbook
paper larger than the silver card stock.
Adhere it with double-sided tape and
apply adhesive letter stickers for the birth
information. Option 2: Print directly
onto the paper using a computer and
printer paper. Create a document and
type in the middle of the document page
the birth name and birth date. Print it
out in portrait mode. Next create another
document; type in the birth length on
one page and the birth weight on another
page. Feed the birth name, birth date
page back into the paper feeder so the
birth length will print on that page.
Then feed the same page through again
so the birth weight will print on it as
well. This takes a little practice to line
up the words. Trim the paper into a
rectangle and adhere it with double-sided
tape to the silver paper.
5. Using a crafts knife on a protected
surface, cut two small diagonal slits in
the top two corners of the ornament.
Cut one end of the ribbon on a diagonal
and feed it through the slit from back to
front. Thread one rondelle bead through
the ribbon. Tie a knot in the ribbon and
feed the loose end back down through
the bead and through the second slit to
the back. Repeat for the other side.

Soft Polka-Dot Stockings

Shown on pages 26–27

WHAT YOU NEED

Tracing paper or copier
¼ yard dotted print fleece fabric
¼ yard white flannel; scissors
⅛-inch-wide cording or satin ribbon
Matching threads

HERE'S HOW

1. Enlarge patterns, *below*, and cut out. With right sides of fleece fabric together, cut 2 from stocking pattern. Cut 2 from white flannel (with bottom on fold) for each cuff. Cut a 1×6-inch piece of fleece fabric to be used for the hanging loop.

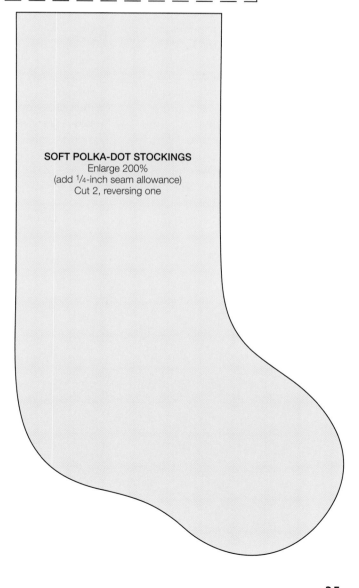

SOFT POLKA-DOT STOCKINGS
Cuff
Enlarge 200%
(add ¼-inch seam allowance)
Cut 2

Place on fold

SOFT POLKA-DOT STOCKINGS
Enlarge 200%
(add ¼-inch seam allowance)
Cut 2, reversing one

Sweet Little Baby

SOFT POLKA-DOT STOCKINGS
Full-Size Patterns

2. Sew stocking pieces together, right sides together, using ¼-inch seam line. Clip curves; turn right side out; press.

3. For loop, fold long edges together, right sides together and stitch using ¼-inch seam. Turn right side out. Fold in half with top raw edges even. Place loop inside stocking at top edge, having loop hang down inside stocking. Baste in place at side edge of stocking.

4. For cuff, print out desired name or writing for stocking from computer font choices or hand letter, as desired. Trace writing onto one cuff piece (with fold at bottom). Couch cording or ribbon by placing trim over letter lines and tacking on trim by stitching with matching thread along side edges of trim and through cuff fabric. Continue to take small, hidden stitches over trim and through cuff fabric to attach trim to cuff. If desired, treat edges with a small dot of clear-drying glue or fabric fray check product to help maintain a crisp cut. *Note:* Names also may be added with purchased letters, machine embroidery, or hand embroidery. See photo, *above*.

5. With right sides together sew side edges of cuff and cuff lining, using ¼-inch seam. Turn right side out and fold in half along bottom fold line. Insert cuff inside stocking with top raw edges even. The right side of the cuff with the writing trim should be facing the wrong side of the front stocking piece. Stitch top seam in a ⅜-inch seam to attach cuff to stocking, also stitching through hanging loop. Flip cuff to outside and lightly press top edge.

Treat Cones
Shown on page 28

WHAT YOU NEED
Tracing paper or copier; pencil
Scissors; crafts glue
Two 7×7-inch pieces of scrapbook
 paper in coordinating colors
 or prints
Clothespin; paper punch; narrow ribbon

HERE'S HOW
Trace the pattern, *below*, and cut out. Trace the pattern onto each piece of the scrapbook papers. Cut out each cone pattern shape. Following the line on the pattern, form the papers into a cone. Run a bead of glue along the edge of the paper to secure. Use the clothespin to hold the cone together until it is dry. Punch a hole through both thicknesses of paper. Thread the ribbon through the holes and knot on the outside. Fill with baby-safe, clean cereal or other item.

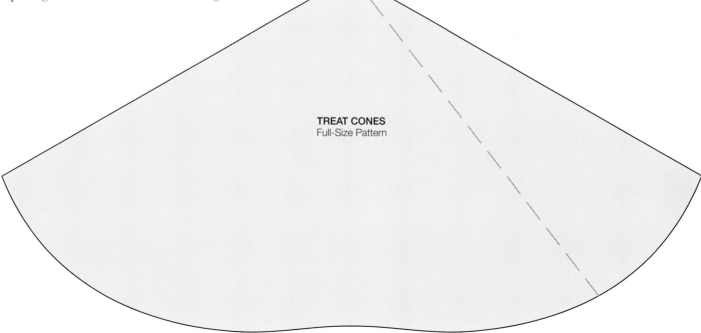

TREAT CONES
Full-Size Pattern

Blanket Trims
Shown on page 29

WHAT YOU NEED
Purchased baby blankets
Narrow gingham ribbon
Jumbo rickrack
Embroidery floss
Needle; straight pins
Sharp scissors

HERE'S HOW
to make the Gingham Ribbon Blanket
Sew gingham ribbon to edge of blanket by straight stitching by machine close to side edges. With two strands of embroidery floss, make lazy daisy stitches along both sides of ribbon. See stitching diagrams, *page 160*. Tie lengths of ribbon into small bows and tack to corners with several hand stitches to secure.

HERE'S HOW
to make the Green Fleece Blanket
Lay jumbo rickrack flat onto purchased blanket about 1½ inches from the outside edge and pin in place. Using two strands embroidery floss, hand-stitch rickrack in place by taking a stitch across the center, from the outside to the center of the trim, creating another zigzag line with the thread. Personalize with the baby's name by using letters printed from computer print. Print out desired size and pin in place onto corner of blanket. With sewing machine use the darning foot and lower the pressure on the presser foot so you guide the machine stitching around the letters. Straight-stitch around each letter through both thicknesses of the fleece blanket. Using sharp, pointed scissors, carefully cut through only the top layer of fleece, cutting very close to the stitching line, to remove the top layer of fabric from inside the letters. The bottom layer of contrasting colored fabric should now be exposed, spelling out the baby's name.

Love Quilt
Shown on page 30

WHAT YOU NEED

*All measurements are for
45-inch-wide fabrics.*

⅛ yard each of cotton fabrics in purple
    and pink pastel colors
⅓ yard yellow cotton fabric
½ yard green cotton fabric
½ yard blue cotton fabric
½ yard light-colored cotton fabric for
    block backgrounds
1⅛ yard light-colored cotton fabric for
    quilt back
35×42-inch piece of thin cotton batting
Sewing thread
Quilting thread
Green, yellow, and pink embroidery
    floss and matching threads
Marking pencil; needle

CUTTING INSTRUCTIONS

Cut all strips across the width of the
fabric.

- Cut 10 2½-inch squares from each of
the purple, pink, yellow, green, and blue
pastel fabrics.
- Cut the following number of 2-inch
squares: 10 purple, 7 pink, 9 yellow,
6 green, 8 blue.
- Cut from background fabric: 40 2½-inch
squares, 10 3½×6½-inch rectangles,
and 20 3½×2-inch rectangles.
- Cut 3 2½-inch strips of yellow fabric for
the border.
- Cut 4 3½-inch strips of green fabric for
the border
- Cut 4 2½-inch wide blue fabric strips
for binding.

HERE'S HOW

1. Using quilt and layout diagram as a
guide, piece together ten 9-patch blocks
from the 2½-inch squares of pastel and
light background fabrics. Piece ten of the
heart blocks using the smaller 2-inch
pastel squares and the light background
fabric rectangles to make a total of twenty
6-inch blocks.

2. Mark triple heart shapes onto the
center of the open area of the heart
block. Thread a needle with all six
strands of embroidery floss and knot the
end of the thread. From back of the heart
block, insert the needle at the bottom of
the heart point, drawing the floss to the
front of the fabric. With one hand lay the
floss along the marked line of the heart.

Machine zigzag-stitch over the floss along this line to couch the thread onto the block. When nearing the end of the point of the heart, draw the floss back to the back side of the fabric and knot in place. Finish machine sewing to the point. You also may use a stem stitch or chain stitch to embroider the heart shapes. (See diagrams, *page 160.*)

3. Arrange the 9-patch and heart blocks in rows, alternating the blocks as shown. Sew blocks together. Add a 2½ inch yellow border to outside and then add the 3½ inch green border.

4. Layer the quilt top, batting, and backing. Baste together. Quilt as desired, or follow the quilting shown on the pictured quilt with stipple quilting in the light background sections, outline stitching around the heart floss shapes, straight lines through the 2-inch squares, stitching in the ditch by the yellow border, and double hearts in the outer green border. Bind the edges with the blue fabric.

LOVE QUILT ASSEMBLY DIAGRAM

BLOCK 1   BLOCK 2

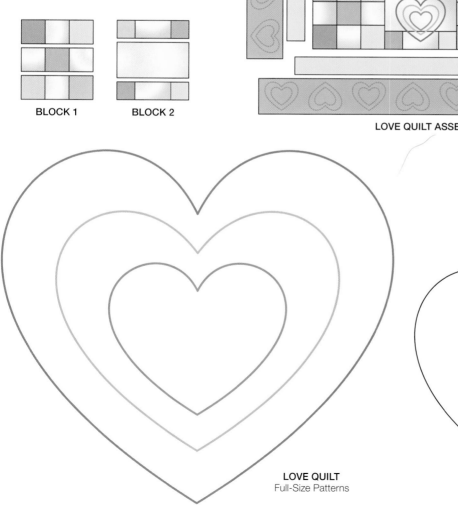

LOVE QUILT
Full-Size Patterns

LOVE QUILT
Full-Size Border Heart
Quilting Patterns

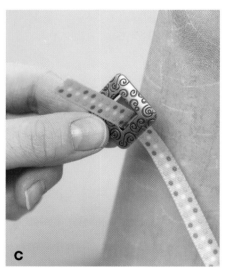

Message Cone Tree

Shown on page 31

WHAT YOU NEED

Three 12×12-inch squares of
coordinating scrapbook paper in
four colors or patterns

Paper glaze such as Aleene's Paper
Glaze

4×9-inch plastic foam cone such as
Styrofoam

5×1-inch round plastic foam disc*

Empty cardboard ribbon spool

Double-sided tape

Tacky glue; pencil; masking tape

Scissors; brush

Access to computer/printer or letter
stickers

Rectangular ribbon charms

4 yards of colorful ribbon to fit ribbon
charms

5-inch length of armature wire

HERE'S HOW

1. Brush two coats of paper glaze onto scrapbook paper allowing drying time between coats.

2. To make the tree base, cut several pieces of scrapbook paper into 1×3-inch strips. Apply double stick tape to the back of the paper strips and adhere the strips (overlapping) to the plastic foam disc. Cut two circles of paper for the top and bottom of disc. Apply with double-sided tape. * If you can't locate a 5×1 inch plastic foam disc you can modify a larger one. Using a compass on a sheet of paper, draw a 5-inch circle. Cut the circle out and pin it to the plastic foam disc using straight pins. Cut the 5-inch circle out of foam using a serrated knife. Use medium grade sandpaper to even the edges of the disc if needed.

3. To make the tree trunk, cut the edges of the cardboard spool off and apply a strip of scrapbook paper using double-sided tape.

4. To make the tree, choose one scrapbook paper and tightly wrap it around the Styrofoam cone. Using a pencil, lightly mark the inside of the paper where the excess is around the bottom of the cone (Photo A). Cut off excess. Secure the paper to the inner portion of the cone using masking tape and tacky glue (Photo B). Secure the paper to the outer portion of the cone using double-sided tape.

Tip: The outside of the cone will look best if you trim the excess paper so the seam in the back of the tree is a vertical, straight line.

5. Attach tree base to tree trunk using double-sided tape. Attach tree trunk to tree using tacky glue. Let dry.

6. Using a word processor, print desired words on scrapbook paper. Practice on printer paper first to adjust font size and type. Thread ribbon charms on ribbon (Photo C). Wrap ribbon around tree and adhere with double-sided tape. Use tape on the back of the entire ribbon and ribbon charm. (This keeps the ribbon and charm in place.) If the tape is narrower than the ribbon you are using, apply the tape to the top edge of the ribbon. (This helps to keep the ribbon from pulling away at the top.) Apply the paper words to the ribbon charms using tape.

7. Using a word processor, print the desired message for the tree base on scrapbook paper. Cut out and apply to base with tape.

8. Coil the five-inch piece of armature wire into a spiral on one end. Insert the straight end through the top of the tree into the cone. Glue in place using tacky glue. Let dry. Using excess ribbon, tie a bow to the spiral.

Sugar Bottles
Shown on pages 32–33

WHAT YOU NEED

Clear glass or plastic baby bottles in varying sizes
Colored sugars (usually used for cookie decorating)
Narrow-edge ribbons

HERE'S HOW

Wash and dry the bottles. Be sure there is no moisture in the bottles. Fill each of the bottles with the desired color of colored sugar. Replace the top. Tie a ribbon around the top of each bottle. Arrange the bottles on a mantel.

Note: Never use decorative bottles to feed baby.

sweets for the season

It's easier than you think to present a homemade, prettily packaged treat to say "thank you" or "Merry Christmas" in the sweetest way. Share these goodies with your favorite people. After all, everyone looks forward to a few special treats during the season!

Whether they've been "nutty" or nice, treat the nut lovers on your list to an amazing batch of **Cinnamon and Sugar Hazelnuts and Brazil Nuts,** *above.* **Pistachio and Dried Cherry Nougat,** *opposite,* is an updated version of an old-fashioned treat. Recipes are on *page 52.*

If you've never made homemade candies, these two choices are good places to start. **White Chocolate Fruit and Nut Candies,** *below,* require only five ingredients and are even easier to make than drop cookies (you don't have to bake them!). Impressive **Double-Chocolate Raspberry Creams,** *opposite,* are simple to make, yet they look anything but. Recipes are on *page 53.*

For **Peppermint Sticks,** *opposite,* simply combine just the right ingredients and pretty them up with cellophane wrap and string. Even if you consider yourself a novice in the kitchen, you can still whip up a batch of delightful **Butterscotch Bars,** *above*—without even turning on the oven! Recipes are on *pages 53–54.*

For some on your gift-giving list, only the most superindulgent chocolate cookie will do. Treat them to **Chocolate-Cherry Pistachio Drops,** *above,* or **Irish Cream Truffle Cookies,** *opposite,* for sophisticated sweets they'll long remember. Recipes are on *page 54.*

Drizzled and dipped in chocolate, **Chocolate-Covered Sandies,** *below,* are so pretty they'll stand in as fancy truffle look-alikes. In spite of their names, Italian-inspired **Almond Sweets,** *opposite,* aren't overly sweet at all. Instead, they're chock-full of rich, buttery, almondy flavor. They'll go great with tea! Recipes are on *page 55.*

Pistachio and Dried Cherry Nougat

Shown on page 42

WHAT YOU NEED

    Butter
    Cornstarch
1½ cups sugar
  1 tablespoon cornstarch
  1 cup light-colored corn syrup
 ½ cup water
  2 egg whites
  1 teaspoon vanilla
1½ teaspoons finely shredded
    lemon peel
 ¾ cup chopped pistachio nuts
 ¾ cup dried tart cherries

HERE'S HOW

1. Line a 9×9×2-inch baking pan with foil, extending foil over edges of pan. Butter foil; sprinkle lightly with cornstarch. Set pan aside.

2. In a 2-quart heavy saucepan combine sugar and the 1 tablespoon cornstarch. Add corn syrup and water; mix well. Cook over medium-high heat until mixture boils, stirring constantly with a wooden spoon to dissolve sugar. (This should take 5 to 7 minutes.) Avoid splashing mixture on sides of pan. Carefully clip a candy thermometer to side of pan.

3. Cook over medium heat, stirring occasionally, until thermometer registers 286°F, soft-crack stage. (This should take 20 to 25 minutes.) Mixture should boil at a moderate, steady rate over entire surface.

4. Remove saucepan from heat; remove candy thermometer from saucepan. In a large mixing bowl immediately beat egg whites with a freestanding electric mixer on medium speed until stiff peaks form (tips stand straight). Gradually pour hot mixture in a thin stream (slightly less than ⅛ inch in diameter) into egg whites, beating with the electric mixer on high speed and scraping sides of bowl occasionally. (This should take about 3 minutes.)

5. Add vanilla. Continue beating with the electric mixer on high speed, scraping sides of bowl occasionally, until candy becomes very thick and less glossy. When beaters are lifted, mixture should fall in a ribbon but mound on itself, then slowly disappear into the remaining mixture. (This should take 5 to 6 minutes.)

6. Immediately stir in lemon peel, nuts, and cherries. Quickly spread mixture in prepared pan. While nougat is warm, score into 2×¾-inch pieces. When candy is firm, use foil to lift it out of pan; remove foil and cut candy into pieces. Wrap each piece in plastic wrap; tie with decorative ribbon. Makes about 48 pieces.

To store: Place wrapped candies in an airtight container and store at room temperature for up to 2 weeks.

Cinnamon and Sugar Hazelnuts and Brazil Nuts

Shown on page 43

WHAT YOU NEED

1¼ cups hazelnuts (filberts)
    (about 6¼ ounces)
    Nonstick cooking spray
  1 cup Brazil nuts (about 6½ ounces)
 ½ cup sugar
  2 tablespoons water
  1 teaspoon ground cinnamon
 ¼ teaspoon cayenne pepper

HERE'S HOW

1. Preheat oven to 350°F. Spread hazelnuts in a shallow baking pan. Bake about 10 minutes or until nuts are toasted and skins flake off easily, stirring nuts once. Place the warm nuts in a clean terry cloth kitchen towel; gently rub nuts together to remove most of the skins. Line the shallow baking pan with foil; lightly coat with cooking spray and set aside.

2. In a large, heavy skillet combine hazelnuts, Brazil nuts, sugar, water, cinnamon, and cayenne pepper. Bring mixture just to boiling over medium-high heat, stirring to dissolve sugar. Reduce heat; boil gently, uncovered, for 2 minutes, stirring frequently.

3. Spread nut mixture in the prepared baking pan. Bake for 5 minutes. Remove from oven and stir to coat nuts with glaze. Cool nut mixture in pan on a wire rack. Break apart any large clusters of the cooled nut mixture. Makes about 3 cups nut mixture.

To store: Place nut mixture in an airtight container and store at room temperature for up to 2 weeks.

White Chocolate Fruit and Nut Candies
Shown on page 44

WHAT YOU NEED
- 4 cups granola with raisins
- 1 cup coarsely chopped cashews, macadamia nuts, or walnuts
- ½ cup snipped pitted dates
- 1¼ pounds vanilla-flavored candy coating, cut up
- 1 14-ounce can sweetened condensed milk

HERE'S HOW
1. Line two large cookie sheets with waxed paper; set aside. In a large bowl combine granola, nuts, and dates; set mixture aside.
2. In a medium, heavy saucepan combine candy coating and condensed milk. Stir over low heat until candy coating is melted and mixture is smooth. Remove from heat.
3. Pour candy coating mixture over the granola mixture; stir gently until coated. Drop by rounded teaspoons onto the prepared cookie sheets. Let stand about 1 hour or until dry. Makes about 72 pieces.

To store: Layer candies between waxed paper in an airtight container; cover. Store at room temperature for up to 3 days. Or freeze for up to 1 month; let stand at room temperature for 30 minutes before serving.

Double-Chocolate Raspberry Creams
Shown on page 45

WHAT YOU NEED
- 1 pound vanilla-flavored candy coating, chopped
- ½ of a 14-ounce can (⅔ cup) sweetened condensed milk
- ¼ cup seedless raspberry preserves
- 4 drops raspberry oil or ¼ teaspoon raspberry flavoring
- 1 pound chocolate-flavored candy coating, chopped
  Chocolate-flavored candy coating and/or cherry-flavored pieces,* melted (optional)

HERE'S HOW
1. In a medium saucepan combine vanilla-flavored candy coating, sweetened condensed milk, and preserves. Cook and stir over low heat until melted. Remove from heat; stir in raspberry oil or flavoring. Transfer to a bowl. Cover; chill for 2 to 3 hours or until just firm enough to shape, stirring once or twice. With damp hands, shape into ¾-inch balls; place on waxed paper-lined 15×10×1-inch pans or trays. Chill for 2 hours.
2. In a medium saucepan melt chocolate-flavored candy coating over low heat until smooth, stirring frequently. Cool

15 minutes. Working with one tray at a time, dip raspberry balls into chocolate mixture to coat; allow excess chocolate to drip back into the saucepan. Place candies on waxed paper-lined cookie sheets; let stand about 15 minutes or until chocolate is set. If chocolate-flavored coating sets up as you are dipping, remelt and cool again before continuing to dip the candies. If desired, drizzle with additional melted candy coating and/or cherry-flavored pieces. Store tightly covered in the refrigerator for up to 3 days. Makes about 72 candies.
*Note: If you are not able to find cherry-flavored pieces, tint melted vanilla-flavored candy coating with red paste food coloring.

Peppermint Sticks
Shown on page 46

WHAT YOU NEED
- 4 ounces bittersweet or semisweet chocolate, chopped
- 1 teaspoon shortening
- ⅔ cup pecans or your favorite nuts, chopped
- 16 3- to 4-inch peppermint sticks

HERE'S HOW
1. In a small heavy saucepan combine chocolate and shortening; stir over low heat just until melted. Transfer to a bowl. Spread pecans on waxed paper.
2. Dip one end of each peppermint stick into melted chocolate and then roll in chopped nuts. Place on a fresh sheet of waxed paper; let stand until set. Wrap each in plastic wrap. Makes 16.

Butterscotch Bars
Shown on page 47

WHAT YOU NEED
- 1 9-ounce package chocolate wafers
- 6 tablespoons butter, melted
- 1 cup creamy peanut butter
- 1½ cups powdered sugar
- 1 11-ounce package (2 cups) butterscotch-flavored pieces
- ¼ cup whipping cream
- ¾ cup chopped peanuts

HERE'S HOW
1. Crush chocolate wafers for a total of 2 cups. In a large bowl stir together butter, peanut butter, and powdered sugar. Stir in chocolate wafer crumbs. Press mixture into the bottom of an ungreased 13×9×2-inch baking pan.
2. In a medium, heavy saucepan combine butterscotch-flavored pieces and whipping cream. Stir over low heat until pieces are just melted. Carefully spoon butterscotch mixture over crumb mixture, spreading evenly. Sprinkle peanuts over butterscotch mixture. Cover and chill at least 2 hours. Cut into bars. Makes 48 bars.
To store: Layer bars between waxed paper in an airtight container; cover and store in the refrigerator for up to 1 week.

Chocolate-Cherry Pistachio Drops
Shown on page 48

WHAT YOU NEED
- 1 cup butter, softened
- ¾ cup granulated sugar
- ¾ cup packed brown sugar

- 1 teaspoon baking soda
- 3 ounces unsweetened chocolate, melted and cooled
- 2 eggs
- 1 teaspoon vanilla
- 2 cups all-purpose flour
- 1½ cups chopped dried tart cherries
- 1 cup pistachio nuts
- 4 ounces white baking chocolate
- 1 tablespoon shortening
- ¼ cup very finely chopped pistachio nuts

HERE'S HOW
1. Preheat oven to 350°F. In a large mixing bowl beat butter with an electric mixer on medium speed for 30 seconds. Add granulated sugar, brown sugar, and baking soda. Beat until combined, scraping sides of bowl occasionally. Beat in the melted unsweetened chocolate, eggs, and vanilla until combined. Beat in as much of the flour as you can with the mixer.
2. Using a wooden spoon, stir in any remaining flour, dried cherries, and the 1 cup pistachio nuts.
3. Drop dough by rounded teaspoons 2 inches apart onto ungreased cookie sheets. Bake about 10 minutes or until edges are firm and cookies are slightly puffed and appear set. Transfer cookies to wire racks and let cool.
4. In a small, heavy saucepan melt white baking chocolate and shortening over low heat, stirring constantly. Drizzle over cookies; immediately sprinkle with the ¼ cup pistachio nuts. Let stand until set. Makes about 48 cookies.

To store: Layer cookies between waxed paper in an airtight container; cover. Store at room temperature for up to 2 days. Or freeze undrizzled cookies for up to 3 months; thaw cookies, drizzle with chocolate, and sprinkle with nuts.

Irish Cream Truffle Cookies
Shown on page 49

WHAT YOU NEED
- 1 egg
- 1 egg yolk
- ½ cup granulated sugar
- 2 ounces semisweet chocolate, melted
- ¼ cup cooking oil
- 1 teaspoon baking powder
- 1 teaspoon vanilla
- 1 cup all-purpose flour
  Powdered sugar
- 2 ounces cream cheese, softened
- ⅓ cup powdered sugar
- 1 ounce semisweet chocolate, melted
- 1 tablespoon Irish cream liqueur or strong brewed coffee
- 1 recipe Chocolate Drizzle

HERE'S HOW
1. In a medium bowl stir together egg, egg yolk, granulated sugar, the 2 ounces melted chocolate, the oil, baking powder, and vanilla. Stir in the flour. Cover and chill dough for 1 to 2 hours or until easy to handle.
2. Preheat oven to 375°F. Shape chilled dough into ½-inch balls. Place balls 1 inch apart on ungreased cookie sheets. Bake for 6 to 7 minutes or until edges are

set. Transfer cookies to a wire rack and let cool. Sift powdered sugar over cooled cookies.

3. For cream filling, in a small mixing bowl combine cream cheese, the ⅓ cup powdered sugar, the 1 ounce melted chocolate, and the liqueur. Beat with an electric mixer on medium speed until combined.

4. To assemble, spread ½ teaspoon of the cream filling onto the flat side of a cookie; top filling with a second cookie, flat side down. Repeat with remaining cookies and cream filling. Drizzle the sandwich cookies with Chocolate Drizzle. Let stand until set. Makes about 45 sandwich cookies.

Chocolate Drizzle: In a small saucepan combine 3 ounces semisweet chocolate and 1 teaspoon shortening. Heat and stir over medium-low heat until melted.

To store: Layer sandwich cookies between waxed paper in an airtight container; cover. Store in the refrigerator for up to 3 days.

Chocolate-Covered Sandies

Shown on page 50

WHAT YOU NEED

   1 cup butter, softened
  ⅓ cup sugar
   1 tablespoon milk
   1 teaspoon vanilla
2¼ cups all-purpose flour
   1 cup chopped almonds, toasted
  12 ounces milk chocolate bar, broken
   3 tablespoons shortening
   3 ounces bittersweet or semisweet chocolate, chopped
     Miniature paper bake cups

HERE'S HOW

1. Preheat oven to 325°F. In a large mixing bowl beat butter with an electric mixer on medium to high speed for 30 seconds. Add sugar. Beat until combined, scraping sides of bowl occasionally. Beat in milk and vanilla until combined. Beat in as much flour as you can with the mixer. Using a wooden spoon, stir in any remaining flour and the almonds. If necessary, knead dough gently with hands until dough clings together.

2. Shape dough into ¾-inch balls. Place 1 inch apart on ungreased cookie sheet.

Bake for 15 to 18 minutes or until bottoms are lightly browned. Transfer cookies to a wire rack and let cool.

3. In a medium, heavy saucepan stir the milk chocolate and shortening over low heat until melted and smooth. Remove from heat; cool 20 minutes. Use a fork to gently dip cooled cookies into chocolate mixture, dipping some completely and some only halfway into the chocolate; allow excess chocolate to drip back into the saucepan. Place cookies on a waxed paper-lined cookie sheet or tray; chill about 30 minutes or until chocolate is firm.

4. In a small heavy saucepan stir the bittersweet chocolate over low heat until melted and smooth. Place cooled melted chocolate in a small plastic bag. Snip one corner of the bag with scissors. Drizzle the chocolate over the coated cookies. Chill for a few minutes until set. Place each in a miniature paper bake cup. Makes about 48 cookies.

To store: Place cookies in an airtight container; cover. Store in the refrigerator for up to 3 days.

Almond Sweets

Shown on page 51

WHAT YOU NEED

2½ cups all-purpose flour
   2 teaspoons baking powder
  ½ teaspoon salt
   3 eggs
  ½ cup granulated sugar
  ½ cup cooking oil
   1 teaspoon vanilla
  ¼ teaspoon almond extract
   1 recipe Almond Icing
     Colored sugar or small multicolored decorative candies (optional)

HERE'S HOW

1. Preheat oven to 350°F. Grease two large cookie sheets; set aside. In a large bowl stir together flour, baking powder, and salt; set aside.

2. In a large mixing bowl beat eggs, granulated sugar, oil, vanilla, and almond extract with an electric mixer on medium speed until combined. Beat in as much of the flour mixture as you can with the mixer. Using a wooden spoon, stir in any remaining flour mixture (dough will be sticky). Drop dough by teaspoons 1 inch apart onto the prepared cookie sheets. Grease teaspoons, if necessary.

3. Bake about 10 minutes or until bottoms are golden and tops are firm. Immediately transfer cookies to a wire rack and let cool. Frost with Almond Icing. If desired, immediately sprinkle lightly with colored sugar or multicolored candies. Let stand until icing is dry. Makes about 36 cookies.

Almond Icing: In a medium bowl stir together 2 cups powdered sugar, ½ teaspoon almond extract, and enough milk (6 to 7 teaspoons) to make a thinner icing.

To store: Layer cookies between waxed paper in an airtight container; cover. Store at room temperature for up to 3 days. Or freeze unfrosted cookies for up to 3 months; thaw cookies and frost.

What better time to start decorating than now!
Try creating your own version of timely ornaments,
jingle bell clocks, and even a holiday wristwatch.

Make your Christmas tree a **Timely Tree,**
opposite, when you fill it with lovely

ornaments that you make using every

possible bit of time. **Ribbon Time Trims,**

above, are created using pretty ribbon and

all kinds of watch part finds. Instructions

for the ornaments are on *pages 66–68*.

time
for christmas

Golden Watch Part Trims, *opposite top,* showcase tiny parts from old watches. You can make simple and elegant Watch Wheel Spheres, *below left,* in no time at all. Tassel Time Ornaments, *below right,* appear to be elegant sundials as they hang in the tree. Make Clock Face Ornaments, *opposite below,* using scrapbook papers in styles and colors that you like. Instructions for all of the ornaments are on *pages 66–68.*

Watch Wheel Sphere

Tassel Time Ornament

Golden Watch Part Trim

Clock Face Ornament

Clock Face Ornament

Make Christmastime in your house even more special by adding touches of color and pretty jingle bells to your favorite clock pieces. Create **Jingle Bell Clocks** for every room. Try a **Spruced-Up-in-Blue Clock,** *opposite,* by tying pieces of blue spruce evergreen onto the clock and adding some blue jingle bells. Choose an old-fashioned white alarm clock and add a touch of painted holly and red jingle bells to make a **Jingle Bell Alarm Clock,** *below.* Instructions and ideas for all of the projects are on *pages 68–69.*

For the favorite holiday room of the house, create

Kitchen Time, *opposite,* by adding fresh greens, jingle bells,

and a bow. Greet your holiday guests with a decorated

Welcoming Clock, *below.* Purchased berries, sheer ribbon,

and jolly jingle bells combine to make this clever look.

Instructions for both projects are on *pages 68–69.*

Find some music-motif ribbon and tie it on a black clock to create

a **Music Lover Clock,** *opposite.* Add some brushed metal jingle

bells to complete the look. Making a **Beaded Holiday Wristwatch,**

above, is easy using a purchased watch face and pretty beads.

Instructions for both projects are on *page 69.*

Ribbon Time Trims

Shown on page 56

WHAT YOU NEED
Gold watch hands and second hands
Wire snips
Watch wheels
½-inch-wide decorative teal ribbon
Strong crafts glue such as Quick Grip
    all-purpose permanent adhesive
Scissors

HERE'S HOW
1. Arrange watch hands and second
hands as desired. Snip extra gears off
watch wheels using wire snips. Use a
small amount of strong crafts glue to
adhere the hands together. Glue a watch
wheel on the back side of the hands to
serve as a loop for hanging the ornament.
Let dry.
2. Cut the ribbon and form a loop behind
watch hands. Glue the ribbon to back
of hands and wheel. Let dry.

Golden Watch Part Trims

Shown on page 59

WHAT YOU NEED
Gold tiny marbles
Small cup
Teal matte-finish ornaments
Assorted miscellaneous watch parts
Glittery silver 3D paint such as
    Scribbles 3D paint
Box with sides

HERE'S HOW
Pour tiny marbles into a small cup.
Generously apply silver 3D paint to the
top of ornament in a "snow-topped"
fashion. Press watch parts into 3D paint.
Hold ornament over box and gently pour
tiny marbles over top of ornament.
Hang the ornament to dry or set in a
secure holder. Pour tiny marbles back
into small cup and repeat instructions
for additional ornaments.

Watch Wheel Spheres

Shown on page 58

WHAT YOU NEED

Assorted watch wheels
Wire snips
Strong crafts glue such as Quick Grip
    all-purpose permanent adhesive
Teal matte-finish ornaments

HERE'S HOW

Remove extra gears from watch wheels using wire snips. Apply a small amount of glue to the center of one watch wheel at a time and adhere to the ornament. (Tip: A wooden toothpick works well to apply a small amount of glue.) Apply wheels randomly in one section of the ornament at a time, allowing glue to dry before decorating other areas of the ornament. Repeat procedure for additional ornaments.

Tassel Time Ornaments

Shown on page 58

WHAT YOU NEED

Scrapbook paper watch face image
Paper glaze such as Aleene's Paper
    Glaze
Brush
Watch hands
Gold tassel; teal glass bead
Gold wire; wire snips
⅛-inch hole punch

HERE'S HOW

1. Brush two coats of paper glaze onto watch face image allowing drying time in between. (This will protect the paper from fingerprints and dust, etc.)
2. Punch a hole in the center of watch face image. Thread tassel loop up through center of watch face. Thread watch hands and glass bead. Using wire snips, cut a piece of wire approximately 3 inches long. Wrap wire around loop just above bead to secure all items threaded on loop. Cut off excess.

Clock Face Ornaments

Shown on page 59

WHAT YOU NEED

Paper Glaze such as Aleene's Paper
    Glaze
Brush
Scrapbook paper clock face image
Gold scrapbook cardstock paper
Assorted watch hands, wheels, parts,
    faces
Gold chain tassel
Wire snips
⅛-inch gold eyelets
⅛-inch eyelet setter and hammer
Gold jump rings
Long nose pliers
Double-sided tape
⅛-inch hole punch
Scissors
Crafts glue

HERE'S HOW

1. Brush two coats of paper glaze to all watch face images allowing drying time between coats. (Photo A, *page 68*). Cut a gold paper back for each of the clock face ornaments. Adhere the back sides with double-sided tape.
2. Lay out clock face images and experiment by adding clock hands, wheels, parts, and faces. Try layering parts for an interesting look. Remove excess gears or protruding metal (if any) with wire snips. Try adding a dangling part, wheel, or gold chain tassel.

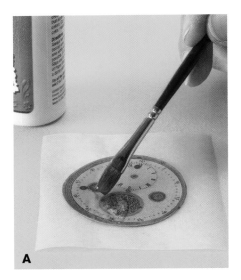

A

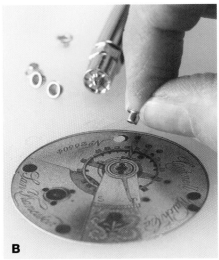

B

C

3. Once you establish the designs for each clock face, prepare to insert a hole and eyelet at the top of each ornament for hanging purposes. Punch a hole in the top of each clock face (Photo B). On a protected surface, insert one eyelet through the hole in the front of the clock face. Turn the clock face over. Rest the setter on the eyelet and use a hammer to tap the top of the setter (Photo C). This will spread the back of the eyelet and secure it to the clock face. Add additional eyelets to the bottom of any clock faces if you are adding wheels or other dangling parts.

4. Glue watch pieces in place on watch face ornaments. Let dry. Add dangling pieces to the bottom of the ornaments using jump rings and long nose pliers.

Jingle Bell Clocks

Shown on pages 60–64

HERE'S HOW

to make the Jingle Bell Alarm Clock
Paint real or artificial holly with white spray paint. Allow to dry. Make a bow from plaid ribbon. Wire red jingle bells to the bow and holly and attach to the white clock.

HERE'S HOW

to make Spruced-Up-In-Blue-Clock
Tie a gold bow and wire it to the top of the clock, tucking fresh greenery under the bow. Wire a string of blue jingle bells to the bottom of the clock.

HERE'S HOW

to make the Kitchen Time Clock
Make a bow from printed ribbon. Wire small gold jingle bells to the center. Add fresh greenery and the ribbon and bells and place on top of the clock.

HERE'S HOW
to make the Welcoming Clock
Wire purchased berries on a garland to the top of an outdoor clock. Add a sheer green bow and green jingle bells.

HERE'S HOW
to make the Music Lover Clock
Make a bow from music-motif ribbon. Add brushed gold jingle bells with wire to the top of a black mantel clock.

Beaded Holiday Wristwatch
Shown on page 65

WHAT YOU NEED
1 mm elastic cord
Scissors
Ruler
Watch face (purchase separately or remove the band from a watch)
Assorted colored glass beads
Strong crafts glue, such as E6000

HERE'S HOW
1. Cut three pieces of elastic, each approximately 10 inches long. The watch face shown has a small bar on each side where the band attaches. The width of the bar allows for several strands of beads. Tie the end of each elastic piece to the bar on one side, leaving a tail. Tie several knots until the elastic feels very secure. Thread several beads, tucking the tail back into the first few beads; trim off the excess elastic. Place a drop of glue on the knot. Let the glue dry.

2. Continue stringing beads onto elastic randomly or by color if desired.
3. After approximately 5 inches of beads are strung, loosely wrap the end of the elastic around the opposite watch bar. Test for fit, then add or remove beads. Finish remaining two strands in the same manner, testing size to fit.
4. With elastic stretched, tie each end on the watch bar, knotting until firm. Tuck the end of elastic back into several beads, stretch, and trim off excess. Place a drop of glue on the knot. Let the glue dry.

handmade gifts and wraps

Everyone on your Christmas list will love the handmade gifts you give this year. Whether you like to sew, quilt, knit, crochet, embroider, or assemble last-minute baskets—you'll find the perfect project to make and give.

What little girl wouldn't love this **Little Lady Bag,** *opposite,* made from snowy white felt? Make it in an evening for the sweet one on your list. The wrap is as much fun as the gift when you present a **Wrapped Organizer Box,** *above.* Instructions for both projects are on *page 80.*

Create a **Christmas Satchel,** *opposite,* in colors of the season for a best friend. She'll love the shape of the purse and clever closure. A colorful scrappy bag is always fun to make. This **Pretty Pieced Purse,** *above,* calls for fabric colors in rich gold and red, but you can make yours with your favorite fabrics. Instructions for the bags are on *pages 80–82.*

A beautiful **Quilted Evening Bag,** *opposite top,* is certain to be a gift she'll treasure. Crochet a **Granny Tote,** *opposite below,* to hold all kinds of digital favorites. Make the tote using ever-so-popular granny squares. Easy to make at the last minute, **Clever Gift Jars,** *left and above,* are fun to make for all ages. Instructions for all of the projects are on *pages 82–84.*

Make pairs and pairs of **Merry Mittens,** *above,* using warm fleece lined with printed flannel. Appliqué a holiday motif to the front of each mitten to complete the look. A creamy winter white **Knit Cable Hat and Scarf,** *opposite,* are easy to make yet look like they took weeks to knit. Instructions for all of the projects are on *pages 84–87.*

Everyone loves stationery so you know they'll appreciate homespun **Printed Fabric Cards,** *opposite bottom.* The set even has a pretty fabric bag holder. Give two gifts at once with a **Quick Scarf Wrap,** *opposite top.* Just tie a purchased scarf around a wrapped gift and add an ornament. Hide some money or a gift card in the **Felted Money Tree,** *above,* and watch the smiles. Instructions for all of these projects are on *pages 86 and 88–89.*

Little Lady Bag
Shown on page 70

WHAT YOU NEED

1 yard white wool felt
3 sheets 8½×11-inch paper for pattern
Tape
Scissors
1 skein red cotton floss
Needle
Red felt
1 button
½ yard cording
Crafts glue

HERE'S HOW

Wash the white felt and let it air-dry. To make the pattern, tape the long end of one sheet of paper to the long end of the next; add the third sheet of paper in the same way. Use scissors to cut the top piece of the pattern into a V that will become the purse flap (see the photo *above*). Place the paper on the white felt and cut all around. Fold the bottom third of the felt over the middle third; stitch the sides together using a blanket embroidery stitch, *page 160*, to create the purse pouch. Also stitch around the V for a cohesive look. Cut four petal shapes from red felt and glue them to the point of the V. Stitch a button in the center to finish. To make the handle, cover the cording with a scrap of white felt, and glue the ends shut. Stitch the handle neatly to the back side of the bag.

Wrapped Organizer Box
Shown on page 71

WHAT YOU NEED

Red organizer box
2-inch-wide silver ribbon
Wire
Silver ornaments
Silver paper and marker for label

HERE'S HOW

Place the gift in the box. Tie the silver ribbon around the box; tie a bow. Wire the silver ornaments into the bow. Use the silver paper and marker to make a name tag and place in the label box area.

Christmas Satchel
Shown on page 72

WHAT YOU NEED

Tracing paper or copier
1 yard fashion fabric

½ yard lining fabric; scissors
⅝ yard lightweight interfacing
Thread to match fabrics
1 set magnetic snaps for purse
1 package dangle shell trim or buttons

HERE'S HOW

1. Enlarge patterns, *opposite*. Cut out all pattern pieces. Iron under ½ inch along side and bottom edges of pockets. Turn top edges of pockets to wrong side ¼ inch and turn again ¾ inch. Edgestitch pocket top hem close to ¼ inch from top. Position pocket on right side of each lining piece. Edgestitch around side and lower edges, reinforcing at top corners.

2. Position magnetic snaps at places marked on bottom of flap and outside front of purse. Attach at markings and reinforce by inserting a square of lightweight cardboard between layers.

3. With right sides together stitch handle lining pieces to front and back purse sections, using ¼-inch seam, stitching around outside edges and inside curve, leaving top short edges of handle open. Clip curved edges; turn right side out. Turn ½-inch seam to inside at handle tops. Butt turned edges together and handstitch handle pieces together over folded edges.

4. With right sides together, stitch side and bottom edges of purse fabric, using ¼-inch seam, starting and stopping at X marked on pattern. Clip curves. Turn right side out.

5. With right sides together stitch lining pieces together, leaving top open, using ¼-inch seam allowance. Trim seam and clip curves. Press ½ inch to back side around top straight edge. Insert lining inside purse. Pin in place and sew through lining and purse along sewing line marked on pattern to attach lining to purse.

6. Turn under straight edge of flap ¼ inch to inside and press. Stitch side and lower curved edges of flap, using ¼ inch seam. Clip curves. Turn and press. Edgestitch close to pressed edges. Pin flap to back of purse, ¾ inch from top center opening. Stitch through tab layers and outside of purse, keeping handle lining free. Stitch close to tab edge and ¼ inch above edgestitching.

7. Sew dangle trim or buttons to stitching line on front of purse.

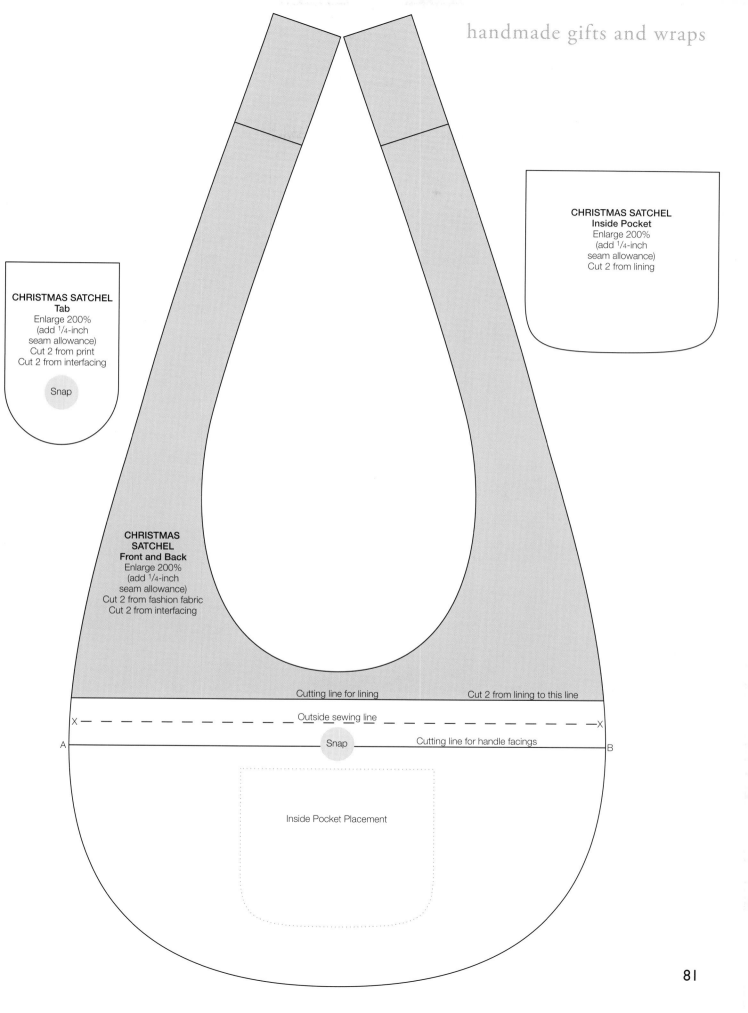

CHRISTMAS SATCHEL
Inside Pocket
Enlarge 200%
(add 1/4-inch
seam allowance)
Cut 2 from lining

CHRISTMAS SATCHEL
Tab
Enlarge 200%
(add 1/4-inch
seam allowance)
Cut 2 from print
Cut 2 from interfacing

Snap

**CHRISTMAS
SATCHEL
Front and Back**
Enlarge 200%
(add 1/4-inch
seam allowance)
Cut 2 from fashion fabric
Cut 2 from interfacing

Cutting line for lining

Cut 2 from lining to this line

X — Outside sewing line — X

A   Snap   Cutting line for handle facings   B

Inside Pocket Placement

Pretty Pieced Purse
Shown on page 73

WHAT YOU NEED
⅔ yard red cotton fabric
¾ yard gold fabric, medium- to
    heavyweight, such as poplin
⅓ yard print cotton fabric
6x7-inch piece striped cotton fabric
¾ yard medium weight iron-on
    interfacing
16-inch length ⅝-inch-wide ribbon
Matching sewing thread; scissors

CUTTING INSTRUCTIONS
Cut the following pieces from the fabrics listed:
- From red fabric: Cut one piece
  16½ inches wide (crossgrain of fabric)
  ×24½ inches long (lengthwise grain of
  fabric) for outside of bag.
  Cut two pieces 7 inch long.
  (lengthwise grain of fabric) ×9 inches
  across (crosswise grain of fabric) for
  inside pocket.
- From gold fabric: Cut one piece
  16½ inches wide (crossgrain of fabric)
  ×24½ inches long (lengthwise grain of
  fabric) for inside lining of bag. Cut
  two pieces 2½ inches wide ×46 inches
  long for handles.
- From print fabric: Cut one piece
  16½ inches wide (crossgrain of fabric)
  ×9¾ inches long (lengthwise grain of
  fabric) for bottom trim of bag.
- From stripe fabric: Cut two pieces
  5¾ inches wide ×6¾ inches long for
  outside pockets.

- From interfacing: Cut one piece
  16½×24½ inches. Cut one piece
  16½×9¾ inches.
- Ribbon: Cut two 8-inch lengths

HERE'S HOW
1. Iron the interfacing to back of large
red fabric piece and print fabric piece to
give more body to the main part of purse
and bottom.
2. Prepare pockets for front and back:
Press under ¼ inch on upper edge. Press
upper edge to inside again ¾ inch to form
facing. Stitch close to folded edge, about
¾ inch from top edge. Pin wrong side of
pocket over right side of red bag piece of
fabric, centering folded edges of pockets
2½ inches from short edges. Baste raw
edges to bag. Repeat with second piece
of striped fabric.
3. Sew handles and bottom section:
Fold handles in half lengthwise with right
sides together. Stitch long edges, using
¼-inch seam allowance. Turn handle right
side out, bringing seam to center on
underside; press. Stitch close to long
outside edges. Pin underside of handles to
bag (over pockets), having raw edges of
handles and pockets even. Stitch close to
long edges of handles, to within ¾ inch
of edge of bag, backstitching to secure.
4. Press under ⅝ inch on long edges of
bottom print fabric. Pin wrong side of
bottom section over right side of
multicolored bag, covering raw edges of
pockets and handles. Stitch close to long
edges, catching pockets and handles.
Baste side edges together.
5. Fold bag with right sides together.
Stitch side edges in ⅝-inch seam and press
open. Press under ½ inch on upper edges
of bag.
6. Prepare facing: Prepare lining pockets
by pressing in ½ inch around side and
bottom edges. Press upper edge to inside
¼ inch. Press upper edge to inside again
¼ inch to form facing. Stitch close to
folded edge, about ¾ inch from top edge.
Place pocket on gold lining piece,
1½ inches down from upper raw edge
of bag. Attach pocket to lining, sewing
close to side and bottom edges.
7. Stitch side seams of facing and press
under upper edge as for bag.
8. Turn bag inside out. At bottom of bag,
fold the fabric point to match up with the

seam line of the bottom print fabric
section, creating a triangle to measure
2 inches from the point. Stitch
perpendicular to the side seam, forming
a line to add depth to the bottom of the
bag. Repeat procedure with the gold
lining section. On the outside, stitch in
the seam line through all thicknesses to
hold the triangular point flat.
9. Put wrong sides of cut ribbon together
and attach by edgestitching close to both
long side edges. Fold ribbon together,
overlapping cut edges. Insert raw edges
between bag and lining at top. Pin in place.
10. With wrong sides together, pin facing
to bag with upper edges even. Stitch
upper edges together, close to folds,
reinforcing by backstitching through
ribbon layers. Turn bag right side out.
Sew button to bag, just above pocket at
side opposite ribbon.

Quilted Evening Bag
Shown on page 74

WHAT YOU NEED
Two 12×19-inch pieces of fabric
One 12×19-inch piece of batting
    (preferably a thin, cotton type)
Two 12×19-inch pieces of lining
50-inch length of ¼-inch cording
Magnetic snap purse closure, Velcro,
    or snaps; scissors
Matching thread; decorative button

HERE'S HOW
1. Place wrong side of one piece of fabric
over the batting and pin in place. Quilt
over all the fabric, following the fabric
design to serve as the quilt lines, or quilt

as desired. After quilting, lay quilted piece of fabric over the remaining piece, right sides together. Trim and square the fabric pieces so they are the exact size (approximately 18×11 inches). Cut triangle pieces from both corners of one end (about 2-inch right triangles) to form the front flap.

2. Place lining right side up on batting side of quilted piece. Fold into thirds and adjust the proportions of the flap and bag, as desired. Mark closures, one on the quilted piece underneath and one on the lining of the top flap. Attach the closures to fabric.

3. Place quilted fabric and lining right sides together. Stitch around all edges, leaving a 4- to 5- inch opening. Clip corners and turn right side out. Press. Turn edges of opening under and press. Stitch closed by hand.

4. Close bag with closures. Place cording at side edges, between layers of fabric, the entire length of the side seam of the bag from the bottom fold to the top where the flap meets. Pin in place. Stitch side seam over cording through front and back quilted fabric layers, using a stitch of some width to catch in cording (elastic zigzag stitch works well).

5. Embellish front of purse with large decorative button.

Granny Tote
Shown on page 74

SKILL LEVEL
Easy

FINISHED MEASUREMENTS
Approx 11½×13"

WHAT YOU NEED
Lion Brand Lion Cotton (Art. 760); 100% cotton, worsted weight; 5 oz. (140 g), 236 yds. (212 m)
1 ball #144 Grape (A)
1 ball #100 White (B)
1 ball #142 Boysenberry (C)
1 ball #174 Lime (D)
Size G/6 (4 mm) crochet hook or size needed to obtain gauge

GAUGE
Granny square = 4" (10 cm) square.
TAKE TIME TO CHECK YOUR GAUGE.

INSTRUCTIONS
FIRST GRANNY (make 4)
Beg in the center with C, ch 2.
Rnd 1: Work 8 sc in 2nd ch from hook; join with sl st in first sc.
Rnd 2: Ch 3 (counts as dc); dc in same sc as joining dc, 2 dc in next sc; *ch 2, 2 dc in each of next 2 dc; rep from * around, ending with ch 2; join with sl st in 3rd ch of beg ch-3. Fasten off.
Rnd 3: With RS facing, join B with a sl st in any corner ch-2 sp.
Ch 3 (counts as dc), in same sp (dc, ch 2, 2 dc). *Sk 2 dc, 3 dc in sp bet 2nd and 3rd dc**, in ch-2 sp (2 dc, ch 2, 2 dc). Rep from * around, ending last rep at **; join with sl st in 3rd ch of beg ch-3. Fasten off.
Rnd 4: With RS facing, join A with a sl st in any corner ch-2 sp. Ch 3 (counts as dc), in same sp (dc, ch 2, 2 dc). *Work 2 dc bet 2nd and 3rd dc, sk 3rd dc, dc bet 3rd and 4th dc, sk 4th dc, dc bet 4th and 5th dc, 2 dc in sp bet 5th and 6th dc**, in ch-2 sp (2 dc, ch 2, 2 dc). Rep from * around, ending last rep at **; join with a sl st in 3rd ch of beg ch-3. Fasten off.
Rnd 5: With RS facing, join C with a sl st in any corner ch-2 sp. Ch 1; *4 sc in ch-2 sp, sc in each of next 10 dc; rep from * around.
Rnd 6: Sl st in FL of each sc around. Fasten off.

SECOND GRANNY (make 4)
With A, ch 2. Work as instructed for First Granny, working Rnds 1 and 2 in A; Rnd 3 in C; Rnd 4 in B; and Rnds 5 and 6 in A.

THIRD GRANNY (make 2)
With C, ch 2. Work as for First Granny with Rnds 1 and 2 in C; Rnd 3 in A; Rnd 4 in B; and Rnds 5 and 6 in C.

FOURTH GRANNY (make 2)
With A, ch 2. Work as for First Granny with Rnds 1 and 2 in A; Rnd 3 in B; Rnd 4 in C; and Rnds 5 and 6 in A.

FIFTH GRANNY (make 2)
With B, ch 2. Work as for First Granny with Rnds 1 and 2 in B; Rnd 3 in D; Rnd 4 in A; and Rnds 5 and 6 in B.

SIXTH GRANNY (make 2)
With A, ch 2. Work as for First Granny with Rnds 1 and 2 in A; Rnd 3 in B; Rnd 4 in D; and Rnds 5 and 6 in A.

SEVENTH GRANNY (make 2)
With D, ch 2.
Work as for First Granny with Rnds 1 and 2 in D; Rnd 3 in A; Rnd 4 in C; and Rnds 5 and 6 in D.

FINISHING
With RS facing, sew squares tog through BL of Rnd 6 in the order shown on the diagrams, right. With RS tog, sew bag sides and bottom edge through BL of Rnd 6.

Top Border
With RS facing, join A at top side seam with a sl st.
Rnd 1: Ch 1, sc in each rem BL around; join with sl st in first sc.
Rnd 2: Ch 3 (counts as dc); dc in each sc around; at end, join with sl st in 3rd ch of beg ch-3.
Rnd 3: Rep Rnd 2.
Rnd 4: Ch 1, sc in same sp as joining, sc in each dc around. At end, sl st in first sc. Fasten off.

7	2	1
3	4	5
6	1	2

2	1	6
5	4	3
1	2	7

Drawstrings (make 1 each of C and D)
With D, ch 3 (counts as 1 dc); dc in 3rd ch from hook. *Ch 2, dc in sp bet last 2 dc; rep from * until drawstring measures approx 36" long.
Weave D drawstring over 4 dc and under 4 dc of first dc rnd on Top Border, beg and ending on the same side. Pull the drawstring so the ends meet. Weave in the loose ends.

Drawstring Clover
Matching end loops on the Drawstring, join D through both loops with a sl st; *ch 3, dc in 3rd ch from hook. Rep from * twice, sl st in same sp as joining. **(Ch 3, dc in 3rd ch from hook) 3 times, sl st in same sp as joining. Rep from ** again. Fasten off.
Make a Drawstring with C and weave it through next dc rnd on Top Border, beg and ending at opposite edge; pull Drawstring so ends meet. Weave in the loose ends.

With C, make a Clover on the Drawstring. Weave in loose ends.

Gift Jars
Shown on page 75

HERE'S HOW
to make the Soap Jar
A square jar works best for this gift. Purchase soap at a dollar or discount store. Unwrap the soap and put in the jar. Add a ribbon and greenery at the top of the jar.

HERE'S HOW
to make the Crayons Jar
Using crayons or colored chalk, write the name of the child on a piece of black scrapbooking paper. Tape it to the jar. Fill the jar with crayons. Add a purchased metallic bow to the top of the jar.

HERE'S HOW
to make the Candy Jar
Start with a quart-size canning jar. Add five or six pieces of rock candy. Cut a circle of colored paper to fit top of the jar. Tie a ribbon around the neck of the jar.

Merry Mittens
Shown on page 76

WHAT YOU NEED
Tracing paper; pencil; scissors
½ yard each of fleece plain or plaid outside mitten fabric and printed flannel lining fabrics

Two 6½-inch squares fabric for cuff
Press cloth; iron; matching threads
Scraps of felt in various shades of green
Santa button (for holly mitten)
20 inches of ¼-inch-wide elastic

HERE'S HOW
1. Enlarge and trace the mitten patterns, *opposite*, onto tracing paper and cut out. Cut shapes from mitten and lining fabrics (reversing pattern for one mitten). Cut out holly shape or tree shape from felt scraps. Appliqué onto front of mittens.
2. Stitch mitten seams, right sides facing and sewing a ¼-inch seam allowance. Stitch the thumb gusset around the curved edge from point A to B. Stitch the inner seam of thumb and palm, tapering to a point at A. Cut the elastic in half. Machine-zigzag over the elastic stretched on the wrong side of the palm/thumb, 3 inches from the top edge. Trim off excess elastic.

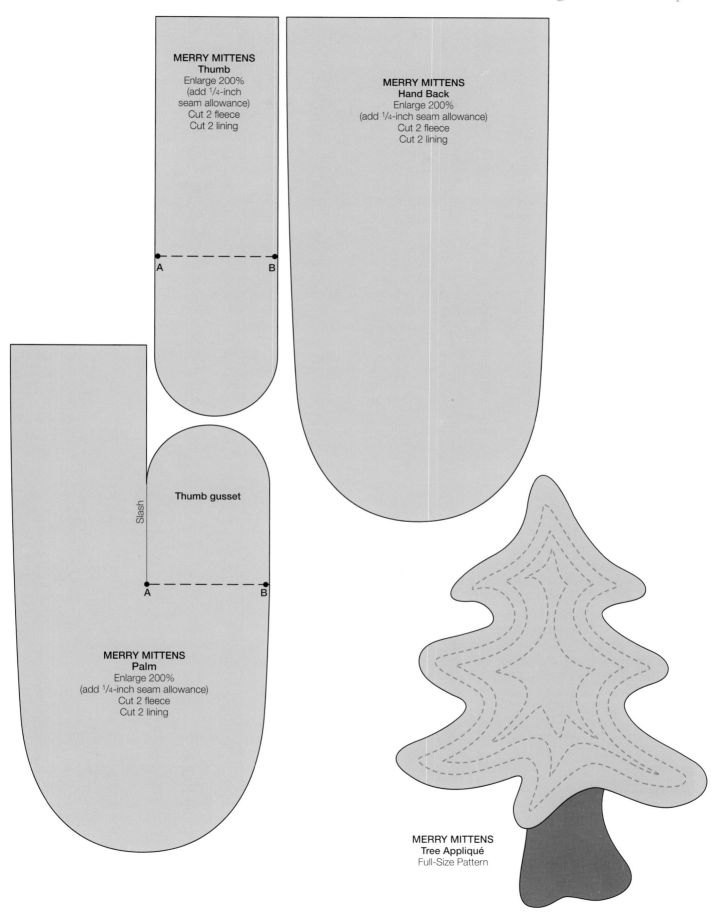

MERRY MITTENS
Thumb
Enlarge 200%
(add ¹/₄-inch
seam allowance)
Cut 2 fleece
Cut 2 lining

A   B

MERRY MITTENS
Hand Back
Enlarge 200%
(add ¹/₄-inch seam allowance)
Cut 2 fleece
Cut 2 lining

Slash

Thumb gusset

A   B

MERRY MITTENS
Palm
Enlarge 200%
(add ¹/₄-inch seam allowance)
Cut 2 fleece
Cut 2 lining

MERRY MITTENS
Tree Appliqué
Full-Size Pattern

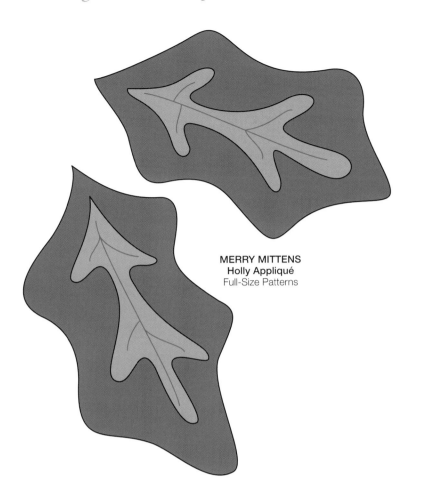

MERRY MITTENS
Holly Appliqué
Full-Size Patterns

Knit Cable Hat and Scarf
designed by Marilyn Losee for Caron
Shown on page 77

SCARF
One size: approximately 7" wide by 54"
long, excluding fringe

WHAT YOU NEED
Caron International's Simply Soft Quick
    (100% acrylic; 3 oz/85 g, 50 yds/46
    m skein):
#0002 Off White, 4 skeins
One pair size US 11 (8 mm)
Cable needle
Yarn needle
Crochet hook size US J-10 (6 mm),
    for Fringe

GAUGE
Gauge is not critical for this project.

STITCHES USED
(Also see Charts, *page 160*)
Seed Stitch (4 sts)
Row 1: *K1, p1; repeat from * once.
Row 2: Knit the purl sts and purl the
knit sts as they face you.
Repeat Row 2 for Seed st.

Right-Slant Cable (panel of 6 sts)
Rows 1, 3 and 7 (RS): Knit.
Row 2 and all WS rows: Purl.
Row 5: C6B: Slip 3 sts to cable needle,
hold to back, knit 3, knit 3 from cable
needle.
Row 8: Purl.
Repeat Rows 1–8 for Right-Slant Cable.

3. Stitch mitten palm to back along sides
and finger curve. Turn right side out.
4. Repeat Steps 2 and 3 for the lining,
leaving an opening for turning in side seam.
5. Stitch ends of each cuff together. Press
seams open. Fold cuff in half, wrong sides
facing and matching raw edges. Ease-
stitch along the top edge of the cuff and
baste to the mitten.
6. Slip mitten into lining, matching side
seams and thumb. Stitch top edge. Slip-
stitch opening in lining closed. Tuck the
lining into mitten and turn cuff down.
Add button embellishment if desired.

Quick Scarf Wrap
Shown on page 78

WHAT YOU NEED
Wrapped present
Long silk scarf
Ornament
Curling ribbon
Scissors

HERE'S HOW
Tie the scarf around the wrapped gift
using a square knot. Tie the ornament
onto the curling ribbon. Tie the ribbon
and ornament into the center of the scarf
knot. Tie a bow with the scarf ends.

Left-Slant Cable (panel of 6 sts)
Rows 1, 3 and 7 (RS): Knit.
Row 2 and all WS rows: Purl.
Row 5: C6F: Slip 3 sts to cable needle, hold to front, knit 3, knit 3 from cable needle.
Row 8: Purl.
Repeat Rows 1–8 for Left-Slant Cable.

HERE'S HOW
Cast on 24 sts.
Begin Cable pattern: Beginning Row 1 of St patterns, * work 4 sts in Seed st, Right-Slant Cable, 4 sts in Seed st, Left-Slant Cable, 4 sts in Seed st. Work even as established until piece measures 54" from beginning, end Row 8 of Cable patterns.
Bind off all sts loosely.

FINISHING
Using yarn needle, weave in ends.

Fringe
Cut strands 16" long. Holding 3 strands together, fold fringe in half. Using crochet hook, * insert hook from WS to RS into first st at corner of one short end, pull through loop (fold), insert ends into loop and pull tight against edge; repeat from *, attaching 5 Fringes evenly spaced across each short end.

HAT
Size: Medium

Hat measures approximately 22" in circumference

WHAT YOU NEED
Caron International's Simply Soft Quick (100% acrylic; 3 oz/85 g, 50 yds/46 m skein):
#0002 Off White, 2 skeins
One pair each size US 9 and 11(5.5 and 8 mm)
Cable needle
Yarn Needle
One circular needle each size US 9 and 11(5.5 and 8 mm), 16" long, for working Hat in-the-round, optional, (see Notes)
Stitch marker, optional, (see Notes)

HERE'S HOW
GAUGE: In Cable pattern, 12 sts (p3, Cable, p3) = 3½"/9 cm and 13 rows = 4"/10 cm

STITCHES USED
(Also see Charts)
Garter stitch (Garter st)
Straight: Knit every row.
Circular: Knit 1 round, purl 1 round.
Reverse St st (Rev St st)
Straight: Purl on RS, knit on WS.
Circular: Purl every round.

Right Slant Cable (Straight)
See Scarf and Chart

Right-Slant Cable (Circular)
Rounds 1–4: Knit.
Round 5: C6B: Slip 3 sts to cable needle, hold to back, knit 3, knit 3 from cable needle.
Rounds 6–8: Knit.
Repeat Rounds 1–8 for Cable.

Note
1. Instructions for Hat are given for working on straight needles, with a Back seam.
2. Instructions for working in-the-round, if they differ, are shown in < >.

HERE'S HOW
Using smaller needles, cast on 60 sts.
<Join, being careful not to twist sts; place a marker (pm) for beginning of round.>
Begin Garter st; work even for 7 rows <rounds>, increasing 3 sts evenly across last (WS) row <last round>-63 sts. Change to larger needles and begin pattern: (RS) P2 (Rev st st), * work Cable across next 6 sts, p3 (Rev St st); repeat from * across <around>, end last repeat p1 (Rev St st), instead of p3.

Work even as established until piece measures 8" from beginning, end with a WS row if working straight.

Shape Crown
Row <Round>1: P2tog, * [k2tog] 3 times across Cable, p3tog; repeat from * across <around>, end p1-29 sts remain.
Work 1 row <round> even (knit the knit sts and purl the purl sts as they face you).
Next Row <Round>: K2tog across <around>, end k1-15 sts remain.
Cut yarn, leaving a 20" <12"> long tail. Using yarn needle threaded with tail, gather remaining sts, and pull tightly to close crown; fasten off securely.
Straight: Sew Back seam.
Using yarn needle, weave in ends.

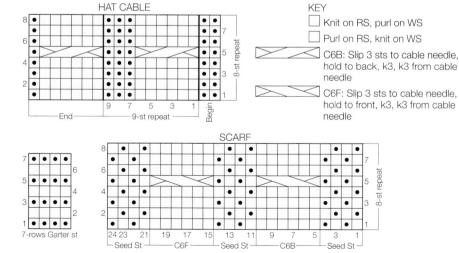

HAT CABLE

KEY
☐ Knit on RS, purl on WS
☐ Purl on RS, knit on WS
C6B: Slip 3 sts to cable needle, hold to back, k3, k3 from cable needle
C6F: Slip 3 sts to cable needle, hold to front, k3, k3 from cable needle

SCARF

handmade gifts and wraps

Printed Fabric Cards

Shown on page 78

WHAT YOU NEED

Blank note cards and envelopes
Fabric scraps to cover 4- to 5-inch note
    cards and a bag that measures
    6×8 inches. (If using the same
    fabric, use about ½ yard of 45-inch
    lightweight cotton fabric.)
Thread; scissors; pinking shears
Crafts glue
Sequins, beads, cording, bows, and
    other embellishments
26-inch length of ribbon

HERE'S HOW
to make the note cards

Flatten out note cards. For each note card
cut a piece of fabric ½ inch larger than
the card on all sides. Using crafts glue,
cover card with a light coat of glue.
Center and press fabric evenly onto card,
smoothing out wrinkles. With paper side
up, trim fabric along card edges with
scissors or a rotary cutter. For the
snowflake card shown, a plain blue strip
of fabric about 1½ inches wide was added
to the bottom edge. Embellish by gluing
on sequins, beads, or bows as desired.

HERE'S HOW
to make the bag

Cut a 13×10-inch rectangle of fabric.
With right sides together fold in half
along the 13-inch length to make a
10×6½ inch section. Stitch the 10-inch
length, pivot at corner, and stitch
across the bottom, using a ½-inch seam
allowance. Turn bag right side out.
Pink across the top edge and press lightly.
Sew ribbon at side seam of bag, 3 inches

from the top pinked edge, by tacking
10 inches into the ribbon length, sewing
into the seam of the bag. Sew by hand or
machine. Add decorative snowflakes at
ribbon ends, as desired.

Felted Money Tree

Shown on page 79

WHAT YOU NEED

One square of green felt or scrap of
    wool felt already washed and dried
Scrap of brown felt
Embroidery floss to match tree color
    and brown floss
Gold metallic embroidery floss
One 12-mm. gold star bead
Gold thread; scissors
6-inch length of gold cording

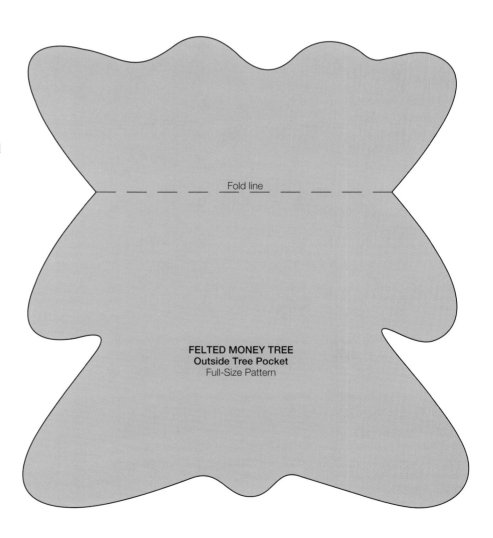

FELTED MONEY TREE
Outside Tree Pocket
Full-Size Pattern

Fold line

HERE'S HOW

1. Copy the full-size patterns, *opposite* and *right*. Cut one of each of the three tree shapes from green felt. Work small stars using staight stitch using gold metallic floss. Cut one small piece from brown felt for trunk. Lay brown trunk piece on top of tree back and sew together using matching brown floss, using the blanket stitch. See stitching diagrams on *page 160*. Lay outside tree pocket piece over the bottom of the tree back piece with the brown trunk.

2. Fold down the top of the outside tree piece and pin in place. Place tree top piece at the top of the tree back piece and pin in place.

3. Using matching tree-colored floss, sew layers together, starting at the top point of the tree, continuing buttonhole stitch around the side edge, sewing through both layers of felt. At the side edge where the wavy curves start, continue the buttonhole stitch around ONLY the top layer of felt until reaching the opposite side edge, then sew through both layers of felt to reach the top point of the tree. Continue sewing through both layers at the side edges, through only the top layer of felt at the wavy front edges, until all edges of the tree are embellished with the buttonhole stitch. A pocket will be formed underneath the tree top piece.

4. Sew the star bead to the tree top, using gold thread. Sew gold cording through all layers at the top to hang the ornament.

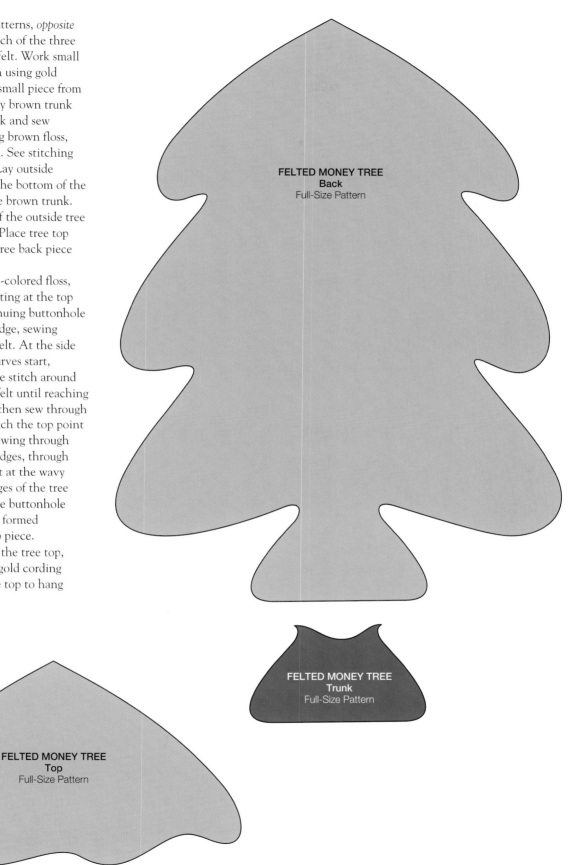

FELTED MONEY TREE
Back
Full-Size Pattern

FELTED MONEY TREE
Trunk
Full-Size Pattern

FELTED MONEY TREE
Top
Full-Size Pattern

warm
welcomes

They'll feel the spirit of the season when they come to your home and are greeted with an entrance all decorated for the holidays as if to say, "Merry Christmas!"

Create a clever **Double Welcome,** *opposite,* by fitting one picture frame inside another. Just add some berries and a pretty bow for a sparkling and welcoming wreath. A **Candle Stand Greeting,** *above,* accents the inside entrance nicely and greets visitors with a bit of warmth as they come to call. Instructions for both projects are on *page 98.*

A creamy white stucco house is **Dressed Up in Pink,** *above,* with ice skates and frosted boxwood trees creating winter white accents.

A mix of pearly pastel ornaments in shades of pink, lavender, and mint sparkles against the white-flocked **Pastel Perfect Wreath,** *opposite and above.* Instructions for making the wreath and suggestions for creating this pastel entrance are on *page 98.*

Give your holiday home a **Playfully Plaid Look**, *opposite,* that is sure to bring them to your door. Create a **Blanket Stocking**, *opposite,* for the main attraction and complete the theme with red jingle bells, sleighs of red pinecones, and swags. Instructions for the stocking and suggestions for the pleasingly plaid entrance are on *pages 98–99.*

Keep it simple with a brilliant **Starry Entrance,** *opposite,* that

is so easy to do. Start with a **Basket of Stars,** *above,* made from

a purchased basket, metal stars you make, and fresh greenery.

Instructions for the Basket of Stars and suggestions for creating

this star entrance are on *page 99.*

Double Welcome
Shown on page 90

WHAT YOU NEED
Two ornate picture frames (one that fits
   just inside the opening of the other)
Strong all-purpose permanent adhesive
Red berry garland
Red ribbon bow
Hot glue gun and glue sticks

HERE'S HOW
Remove backing and glass from both
picture frames. Glue frames together.
Let dry. Lay berry garland around the
edge between the two frames. Hot-glue
in place. Hot-glue a red ribbon bow to
the bottom middle section of the frame
using a hot glue gun.

Candle Stand Greeting
Shown on page 91

WHAT YOU NEED
Two purchased ceramic plant stands
Paint for painting stands
Gold rubbing compound such as
   Rub 'n Buff

Glitter; crafts glue
Red jewels
Glue suitable for gluing to candles
Candle to fit the stand

HERE'S HOW
Paint the plant stands. Allow to dry.
Use the gold rub to rub over the painted
pieces. Dust with glitter. Glue the jewels
onto the finished piece using the crafts
glue. Glue the jewels to the candle using
the candle glue. Stack the stands and
place a candle in the top stand.

Dressed Up in Pink
Shown on page 92

Overall entrance ideas: To keep an entry
feeling open and airy like this one, avoid
garland around the doorway. Instead,
drape swags along railings and choose a
wreath that mimics your door's character,
making the entry a focal point. If you
can't find flocked greens at a local tree
farm, use spray-on flocking. Spray-on
flocking is available at most crafts stores.
Arrange boxwood branches in plastic
foam tree forms and anchor them in the
bottoms of white-painted tin buckets.
A pair of white ice skates finishes the
winter-wonderland look.

Pastel Perfect Wreath
Shown on page 93

WHAT YOU NEED
Purchased real or artificial wreath
Spray snow
Pastel-colored ornaments
24-gauge wire; wire cutters

HERE'S HOW
Wire the ornaments into the wreath,
twisting the wire to the back. Cut off any
excess wire using wire cutters. Spray
wreath and ornaments with spray snow.
Allow to dry.

Playfully Plaid Look
Shown on page 94–95

Overall entrance ideas: A red-brick
house with a green front door lends itself
to the season's traditional hues. Play up
the classic red and green colors with pine
branches and plaid accents. Frame the
door by securing fresh garland around it.
Attach large, red spray-painted pinecones
to add a touch of standout color. A
wheelbarrow holds goodies for a sledding
party, but a wagon, sled, or sleigh would
work just as well. On the porch, two
small trees give balance. Tuck fresh-cut
pine branches into inexpensive artificial
trees. Line the walk with decorative lights
such as our red jingle bells.

Blanket Stocking
Shown on page 94

WHAT YOU NEED
Tracing paper or copier
Pencil
Scissors
Purchased woven wool plaid blanket
   with fringe
Thread to match blanket color
Evergreens, eucalyptus, and plaid-
   wrapped packages

HERE'S HOW

Enlarge the pattern, *below*, onto tracing paper and cut out. Fold the blanket in half, right sides together with the fringe at the top. Place the pattern on the blanket with the top of the pattern along the fringe. Cut out. Stitch around the stocking using a ½-inch seam. Turn and press. Turn the fringe cuff to the outside of the stocking forming the cuff. Tuck evergreens, eucalyptus, and plaid-wrapped packages inside before hanging stocking on the door.

Starry Entrance

Shown on pages 96–97

Overall entrance ideas: The exposed wood beams and wood front door on a Tudor-style house are perfect for this starry entrance. A tree branch and forest greens keep the décor simple, while silvery stars and tin tree luminaries add a hint of holiday sparkle. Outline the door in garland, then attach silver accents. If your door has no built-in hooks, tap thin nails into the frame's corners and into porch supports. Wire garland to the nails. Spray greens with tin or silver spray-painted stars. We cut stars from tin sheets available at local crafts stores. Thin tin strips (careful—they can be sharp!) naturally spiral into shooting star trails. For a unique holiday tree, place a 4- to 5-foot fallen tree branch in a tin pail anchored with floral clay, rocks, and faux snow. Dangle ornaments on its branches. A basket bursting with cedar, juniper, and stars hangs below the door's window.

**BASKET OF STARS
Star Patterns**
Full-Size Patterns

Basket of Stars

Shown on page 96

WHAT YOU NEED

Tracing paper; pencil
Three 10×10-inch pieces of tin sheets, available at crafts stores; tin snips
Rectangle-shaped basket with flat edge on one side
Cedar and juniper greens; wire

HERE'S HOW

1. Trace or copy the full-size star shapes, *above*. Cut out the shapes. Place the pattern on one of the tin sheets and draw around it using a pencil. Cut out using the tin snips. (Be careful—tin is sharp!)
2. Set aside. Fill the basket with the greens. Wire the back and hang on the door. Add the tin stars to the greens.

BLANKET STOCKING
Enlarge 400%
(add ¼-inch seam allowance)
Cut 2, reversing one

party fare

Whether you're off to make merry at a grand-scale potluck or keeping it cozy at home, these holiday-special appetizers and desserts will add much joy to the occasion.

Party foods infused with cheese always satisfy! Stir this luscious ingredient into **Beer and Cheddar Fondue,** *opposite.* Or melt it with almonds and bacon onto irresistible **Bacon-Cheese Melts,** *above.* Either choice will garner rave reviews. Recipes are on *page 110.*

Sometimes the most classic appetizers, such as stuffed mushrooms and cocktail weenies, get the most attention—that's especially true when you imbue them with new twists and turns. **Maple-Mustard Cocktail Sausages,** *below,* and **Horseradish-Stuffed Mushrooms,** *opposite,* are familiar enough to be approachable, but newfangled enough to turn heads. Recipes are on *pages 110–111.*

Heading to a potluck? Let **Curry-Glazed Pork Ribs,** *above,* tag along in your slow cooker—it will help them stay warm on the way, then you can heat them up once you arrive. You can bet nobody else brings a bruschetta that's as Christmas- inspired as **Double Cranberry Crostini,** *opposite.* Recipes are on *page 111.*

Ever make a showstopping holiday dessert only to hear everyone complain they're too full to enjoy it? There's always room for bubbly and refreshing liqueur-spiked **Raspberry-Chocolate Fizz,** *opposite top*. Dainty servings of **Rice Pudding with Lingonberries,** *opposite bottom,* and darling **Mini Snowball Cakes,** *below*, come in just the right size after a heavy meal. Recipes are on *page 112.*

Set to serve a crowd, showy and snowy **Festive Coconut-Lemon Cake,** *opposite,* gets a welcome tingle from a lemon curd filling. It's easy because it starts with a mix. Creamy, chocolaty, and rich **Tiramisu Brownie Trifle,** *above,* deserves a special place in the spectacular desserts hall of fame. Recipes are on *page 113.*

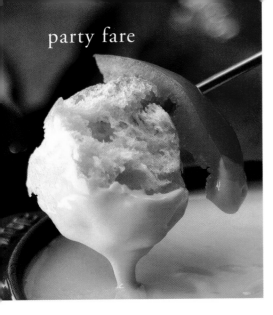

Beer and Cheddar Fondue

Shown on page 100

WHAT YOU NEED

- 1 clove garlic, halved
- 1 12-ounce can or bottle beer
- ½ teaspoon instant chicken bouillon granules
- 2 tablespoons cornstarch
- 2 tablespoons cold water
- 8 ounces sharp cheddar cheese, shredded (2 cups)
- 4 ounces American cheese, shredded (1 cup)
  Assorted dippers, such as French or Italian bread cubes, soft pretzels, breadsticks, red sweet pepper pieces, and/or broccoli florets

HERE'S HOW

1. Rub the bottom and sides of a heavy metal fondue pot* with the garlic halves; discard garlic. In the fondue pot combine beer and bouillon granules. Bring to boiling over medium-high heat.

2. In a small bowl stir together the cornstarch and the cold water; add all at once to beer mixture. Cook and stir until thickened and bubbly. Reduce heat to medium-low. Gradually stir in shredded cheeses, stirring after each addition until cheeses are melted.

3. Place fondue pot over fondue burner. Serve immediately with desired dippers. Spear dipper with a fondue fork or wooden skewer; dip into cheese mixture, swirling to coat. (Fondue will thicken as it holds over the burner.) Makes 10 to 12 servings.

*Note: If you want to use a ceramic fondue pot, use a medium saucepan to prepare as directed through Step 2. Transfer cheese mixture to ceramic fondue pot and continue as directed in Step 3.

Bacon-Cheese Melts

Shown on page 101

WHAT YOU NEED

- 1 16-ounce loaf party rye or pumpernickel bread
- 2 cups shredded sharp cheddar cheese (8 ounces)
- 8 slices bacon, crisp-cooked, drained, and crumbled
- 1 cup mayonnaise
- ½ cup very finely chopped onion (1 medium)
- ¼ cup slivered almonds, toasted* and chopped
- 1 teaspoon Worcestershire sauce
- ¼ teaspoon salt
- ¼ teaspoon ground black pepper
  Fresh thyme sprigs (optional)

HERE'S HOW

1. Preheat oven to 375°F. Place bread slices in a single layer on one or two large baking sheets. Bake about 5 minutes or until bread is toasted.

2. Meanwhile, in a medium bowl combine cheese, bacon, mayonnaise, onion, almonds, Worcestershire sauce, salt, and pepper. Spread each piece of bread with a scant 1 tablespoon of the cheese mixture. Replace on baking sheet(s).

3. Bake for 5 to 7 minutes or until cheese melts. If desired, top with fresh thyme sprigs. Serve immediately. Makes about 45 appetizers.

*Note: To toast nuts, spread them in a single layer in a shallow baking pan. Bake in a 350°F oven for 5 to 10 minutes or until nuts are golden brown, watching carefully and stirring once or twice.

Maple-Mustard Cocktail Sausages

Shown on page 102

WHAT YOU NEED

- ½ cup bottled chili sauce
- ⅓ cup pure maple syrup or maple-flavored syrup
- 2 tablespoons Dijon-style mustard
- 1 tablespoon packed brown sugar
- 1 teaspoon cider vinegar
- 2 16-ounce packages small, cooked smoked sausage links
  Assorted crackers (optional)
  Assorted cheeses (optional)

HERE'S HOW

1. For sauce, in a large bowl stir together the chili sauce, maple syrup, mustard, brown sugar, and vinegar until combined. Add sausages, stirring to coat. Transfer the sausage mixture to a 1½- or 2-quart slow cooker.

2. Cover and cook on low-heat setting for 4 to 5 hours or on high-heat setting for 2 to 2½ hours. If no heat setting is available, cook for 3 hours. Serve immediately or keep warm, covered, on warm setting or low-heat setting (if available) for up to 2 hours. Serve with a slotted spoon or decorative toothpicks. If desired, serve with assorted crackers and cheeses. Makes 32 appetizer servings.

Horseradish-Stuffed Mushrooms

Shown on page 103

WHAT YOU NEED

- 24 large (1½ to 2 inches in diameter) white or cremini mushrooms
- 3 tablespoons olive oil
- ⅓ cup chopped onion
- 2 3-ounce packages cream cheese, cut up
- 3 to 4 teaspoons prepared horseradish
  Garnishes, such as snipped fresh chives, Italian (flat-leaf) parsley, or basil, and/or cooked bacon pieces

HERE'S HOW

1. Preheat oven to 425°F. Clean mushrooms and remove the stems. Chop stems; reserve ¾ cup of the stems (discard remaining stems). Lightly brush mushroom caps using 1 tablespoon of the olive oil. Place mushroom caps, stem sides down, in a 15×10×1-inch baking pan. Bake for 5 minutes. Carefully place mushroom caps, stem sides down, on a double thickness of paper towels to drain while preparing filling. Set aside.

2. For filling, in a large skillet cook chopped mushroom stems and onion in remaining 2 tablespoons olive oil over medium heat about 8 minutes or until onion is tender, stirring occasionally. Remove from heat; add cream cheese and horseradish to mushroom mixture in hot skillet. Let stand 2 minutes. Stir until combined.

3. Place mushroom caps, stem sides up, in the same baking pan. Using a spoon, mound filling into mushroom caps. Bake for 8 to 10 minutes or until heated through and cheese is browned slightly. Sprinkle with garnishes. Makes 24 mushrooms.

Curry-Glazed Pork Ribs

Shown on page 104

WHAT YOU NEED

- 2½ pounds pork loin back ribs, sawed in half across the bones*
- ½ cup mango chutney
- ¾ cup apple juice or apple cider
- 2 tablespoons quick-cooking tapioca, crushed**
- 2 teaspoons curry powder

HERE'S HOW

1. Cut ribs into single-rib portions. Place ribs in a 3½- or 4-quart slow cooker. In a small bowl cut any large pieces of chutney; stir in apple juice, tapioca, curry powder, ¼ teaspoon salt, and ⅛ teaspoon ground black pepper. Pour over ribs.

2. Cover and cook on low-heat setting for 5 to 6 hours or on high-heat setting for 2½ to 3 hours. Makes about 24 ribs.

* Note: Order ahead of time and ask the butcher to saw them in half crosswise.

**Note: Crush with a mortar and pestle.

Double Cranberry Crostini

Shown on page 105

WHAT YOU NEED

- 1 recipe Cranberry-Ginger Chutney
- ⅓ cup dried cranberries
- 2 3-ounce packages cream cheese, softened
- 2 tablespoons chopped pecans, toasted (see note, *page 110*)
- 1 teaspoon finely chopped, peeled fresh ginger
- 1 teaspoon lime juice
- 1 16-ounce loaf baguette-style French bread
- 4 ounces thinly sliced smoked turkey or ham

HERE'S HOW

1. Prepare Cranberry-Ginger Chutney; set aside to cool. Preheat oven to 375°F. Place dried cranberries in a small bowl with enough boiling water to cover; cover and let stand 15 minutes. Drain berries well.

2. For cranberry-cheese mixture, in a medium bowl beat cream cheese until smooth. Beat in drained cranberries, pecans, ginger, and lime juice; set aside.

3. Slice baguette diagonally into ½-inch-thick slices. Place in a single layer on one or two large baking sheets. Bake for 6 to 8 minutes or until edges just start to brown. Cool slightly. Cut turkey into about 30 pieces to fit on bread slices. Spread bread with cranberry-cheese mixture. Top each with a piece of turkey. Dollop with Cranberry-Ginger Chutney. Makes about 30 appetizers.

Cranberry-Ginger Chutney: In a medium saucepan combine 1½ cups cranberries; ¾ cup packed brown sugar; ⅓ cup dried apricot halves, chopped; ⅓ cup golden raisins; 2 tablespoons finely chopped, peeled fresh ginger; 2 tablespoons cranberry juice; ¾ teaspoon ground cardamom; and ¼ teaspoon cayenne pepper. Cook over medium heat, stirring constantly, until sugar is dissolved. Cook, uncovered, for 3 to 4 minutes more or until cranberries pop, stirring occasionally. Transfer to a bowl; let stand about 1 hour or until completely cool. Cover and chill for up to 1 week.

Raspberry-Chocolate Fizz

Shown on page 106

WHAT YOU NEED

- ½ cup chocolate-flavored syrup or chocolate liqueur
- ½ cup raspberry liqueur or raspberry syrup
- 16 scoops raspberry-flavored ice cream, vanilla ice cream, or black raspberry-chocolate ice cream (4 cups)
- 4 cups raspberry-flavored carbonated beverage or cream soda
  Grated chocolate (optional)
  Chocolate-covered peppermint or candy sticks

HERE'S HOW

1. For each serving, pour 2 teaspoons of the chocolate syrup in the bottom of a tall pilsner glass or other tall glass. Drizzle 2 teaspoons of the raspberry liqueur down the sides of each glass.
2. Add 2 scoops ice cream (½ cup total) to each glass. Drizzle ice cream with an additional teaspoon raspberry liqueur and an additional teaspoon chocolate syrup.*
3. Slowly pour ½ cup raspberry beverage over ice cream. If desired, garnish with grated chocolate. Serve with chocolate-covered candy sticks. Makes 8 servings.
*Make-ahead directions: Prepare beverages through Step 2. Cover and freeze glasses for up to 4 hours before adding carbonated beverage.

Rice Pudding with Lingonberries

Shown on page 106

WHAT YOU NEED

- 1 quart whole milk (4 cups)
- 1 quart half-and-half (4 cups)
- 1 cup sugar

- 2½ cups uncooked arborio rice (do not use long grain rice)
- ½ teaspoon salt
- 4 to 6 whole cloves
- 1 vanilla bean, split
  Purchased lingonberry sauce

HERE'S HOW

1. In a 4½- or 5-quart slow cooker stir together milk, half-and-half, sugar, rice, and salt. Tie cloves in a 100-percent-cotton cheesecloth bag. Add vanilla bean and cloves to rice mixture. Cover and cook on low heat setting for 5 to 5½ hours or until rice is just done. (No need to stir during cooking, but do stir once the pudding is removed from heat.)
2. Remove and discard vanilla bean and cloves. Reserve half of the rice pudding for another use; cover and chill for up to 3 days. Let remaining rice pudding stand 15 to 30 minutes before serving. (If pudding gets too thick while standing, stir in some milk to make desired consistency.) Spoon half of the pudding into small glasses or dessert dishes. Top with a small spoonful of lingonberry sauce. Top with remaining rice pudding. Serve warm or chilled in small glasses. Makes 16 servings.

Mini Snowball Cakes

Shown on page 107

WHAT YOU NEED

  Nonstick cooking spray
- 1 package 1-layer-size white cake mix
- ½ cup canned eggnog

- 1 egg
- 1 teaspoon vanilla
- ⅛ teaspoon ground nutmeg
- ¾ cup shredded coconut
  Red or green food coloring (optional)
- 1 3-ounce package cream cheese, softened
- 2 tablespoons butter, softened
- ¾ cup powdered sugar
- ½ teaspoon vanilla
- 1 to 2 tablespoons canned eggnog

HERE'S HOW

1. Preheat oven to 350°F. Lightly coat thirty-six 1¾-inch muffin cups with nonstick cooking spray (or line muffin cups with miniature paper bake cups); set aside.
2. In a medium mixing bowl combine cake mix, the ½ cup eggnog, egg, the 1 teaspoon vanilla, and nutmeg. Beat with an electric mixer on low speed just until combined. Beat on medium speed for 2 minutes until well combined, scraping side of the bowl often. Divide batter evenly among the muffin cups, filling each about two-thirds full (about 1 rounded teaspoon in each). Bake for 10 to 12 minutes or until a wooden toothpick inserted in centers comes out clean. Cool mini cupcakes in pans on wire racks for 5 minutes. Remove mini cupcakes from muffin cups and place on a wire rack. Cool completely.
3. To tint coconut, if desired, in a small resealable plastic bag combine some of the coconut and several drops of red or green food coloring. Seal bag. Using your hands, knead the bag until all of the

coconut is tinted, adding more food coloring as necessary to reach desired color. Set tinted coconut aside.

4. For frosting, in a medium mixing bowl beat cream cheese and butter with an electric mixer on medium speed until well combined. Beat in powdered sugar and the ½ teaspoon vanilla. Beat in enough eggnog (1 teaspoon at a time) until frosting reaches dipping consistency.

5. Dip tops of cooled mini cupcakes in cream cheese frosting. Immediately dip frosted tops into plain or tinted coconut. Set the mini cupcakes upright. Makes 36 mini cupcakes.

Festive Coconut-Lemon Cake
Shown on page 108

WHAT YOU NEED
    1   package 2-layer-size white cake mix
    1   teaspoon coconut extract
    ½   cup lemon curd
    1   12-ounce container frozen whipped dessert topping, thawed
    ½   cup shredded coconut
    ½   cup pistachio nuts, chopped
    ¼   cup shredded coconut, toasted*
    2   tablespoons pistachio nuts, chopped
        Lemon peel curls (optional)

HERE'S HOW
1. Preheat oven to 350°F. Grease two 9×1½-inch round baking pans. Prepare cake mix according to package directions, except add coconut extract to cake batter. Bake according to package directions. Cool cake in pans on wire racks for 10 minutes. Remove cake layers from pans. Cool thoroughly on wire racks.

2. To assemble, place one cake layer on a serving platter. In a small bowl fold together lemon curd and ½ cup of the whipped dessert topping; chill remaining topping until ready to use. Stir ½ cup shredded coconut and ½ cup pistachio nuts into the lemon curd mixture. Spread lemon curd mixture on top of cake layer. Top with remaining cake layer. If desired, chill for 24 hours before frosting.

3. Frost top and sides of cake with remaining whipped dessert topping. Serve at once or refrigerate for up to 4 hours. Before serving, sprinkle top of cake with ¼ cup toasted coconut, 2 tablespoons pistachio nuts, and, if desired, lemon peel curls. Makes 12 servings.

*Note: To toast coconut, spread in a single layer in a shallow baking pan. Bake in a 350°F oven for 5 to 10 minutes or until pieces are golden brown, watching carefully and stirring once or twice.

Tiramisu Brownie Trifle
Shown on page 109

WHAT YOU NEED
    1   recipe Fudgy Coffee Brownies
    ⅓   cup water
    ¼   cup granulated sugar
    2   tablespoons instant espresso coffee powder or instant coffee crystals
    1   3-ounce package ladyfingers, split
    1   8-ounce package cream cheese, softened
    ½   of an 8-ounce carton dairy sour cream
    ¼   cup coffee liqueur or 1 teaspoon instant espresso coffee powder or instant coffee crystals dissolved in ¼ cup warm water
    ½   cup powdered sugar
    1   teaspoon vanilla
    1   cup whipping cream
    1   recipe Coffee Whipped Cream
        Chocolate curls (optional)

HERE'S HOW
1. Prepare Fudgy Coffee Brownies and cool completely. For coffee syrup, in a small saucepan combine ⅓ cup water, granulated sugar, and 2 tablespoons espresso coffee powder. Cook over medium heat until boiling. Boil, uncovered, 1 minute. Remove from heat and cool.

2. Brush flat sides of ladyfingers with cooled coffee syrup; drizzle any remaining syrup over the brownies. Coarsely crumble the brownies. Layer half of the brownies in the bottom of a clear 3-quart soufflé dish or trifle bowl.

3. In a large mixing bowl beat cream cheese with an electric mixer until light and fluffy. Beat in sour cream, coffee liqueur, powdered sugar, and vanilla until combined. Gradually add whipping cream to cream cheese mixture, beating on medium to high speed until thickened. Spoon half of the whipping cream mixture over the brownies. Top with ladyfingers. Spoon remaining whipping cream mixture over the ladyfingers.

4. Layer the remaining crumbled brownies over the whipping cream layer. Cover and chill for 2 to 24 hours. To serve, drop Coffee Whipped Cream by spoonfuls over brownie layer. If desired, garnish with chocolate curls. Makes 12 servings.

Fudgy Coffee Brownies: Preheat oven to 350°F. Grease a 9×9×2-inch baking pan; set aside. In a medium saucepan melt ½ cup butter and 3 ounces unsweetened chocolate, coarsely chopped. Remove from heat. Stir in 1 tablespoon instant espresso coffee powder or instant coffee crystals; cool 15 minutes. Stir in 1 cup granulated sugar and 2 eggs, beating well with a wooden spoon. Combine ⅔ cup all-purpose flour and ¼ teaspoon baking soda; stir into chocolate mixture. Spread in prepared pan. Bake for 25 minutes.

Coffee Whipped Cream: Chill a medium mixing bowl and the beaters of an electric mixer. In the chilled bowl combine 1 cup whipping cream, 2 tablespoons granulated sugar, and 2 tablespoons coffee liqueur or cooled brewed espresso coffee. Beat on medium speed until soft peaks form.

white christmas

Decorate with pure and simple, ever-popular winter white for a most elegant Christmas this year.

If snow isn't in the forecast, create your own

Snowy Tree, *opposite,* with just a little paint

and some snowy spray. Simple and elegant,

a **Pretty Potted Candle,** *above,* serves as a

centerpiece or as a warm glowing welcome

on a table or mantel. Instructions for both

projects are on *page 122.*

Naturally beautiful starfish are the inspiration for a holiday **Starfish Wreath,** *opposite,* created using starfish from the sea, white paint, and fine sparkling glitter. Arrange the pretty wreath on a white shelf with jars of shells and white garland. Instructions for making the wreath are on *page 122.*

Create **Mirror Rosette Embellished White Pillars,** *above,* from clear glass holders and beautiful crystal beads. The trio is a perfect focal point for a holiday mantel or buffet. Winter white 3-D **Fabric Snowflake Ornaments,** *opposite,* are cleverly constructed by layering cut-out pieces. Instructions for both projects are on *pages 123–126.*

Glass ornaments that open and close are the inspiraton for these beautiful **White Crystal Ornaments,** *above.* Top off the tree in white with a **White Beaded Tree Topper,** *opposite above,* made from purchased pearl sprays. Pure white roses are strung with green glass beads to make a lovely **Bead and Rose Garland,** *opposite below.* Instructions for all of the projects are on *pages 126–127.*

Snowy Tree
Shown on page 114

WHAT YOU NEED
Galvanized pail
Small rocks
Purchased small artificial tree
White spray paint
White spray snow
Purchased white star ornaments

HERE'S HOW
Fill the pail with the small rocks. Place the tree in the rocks. Spray the artificial tree with a layer of white spray paint, allowing the paint to spill over onto the rocks and pail like snow. Allow to dry. Spray the tree with spray snow allowing the snow to spill over. Allow to dry. Dangle white-painted star ornaments from tree limbs.

Pretty Potted Candle
Shown on page 115

WHAT YOU NEED
Terra-cotta pot
Spray paint in desired color
White glitter; white icy floral filler
Candle to fit pot

HERE'S HOW
Spray the pot with the paint. Dust with glitter. Allow to dry. Fill the pot with floral filler. Add the candle. Dust with glitter again.

Never leave a burning candle unattended.

Starfish Wreath
Shown on pages 116–117

WHAT YOU NEED
9-inch purchased plastic foam wreath
Natural starfish (available at crafts and
    shell stores)
White spray paint
Crafts glue suitable for gluing to the
    wreath
Paintbrush
White glitter

HERE'S HOW
1. Spray the wreath and the starfish with the white spray paint.
2. Allow to dry. Lay the wreath on a flat surface and glue the starfish onto the wreath. Allow to dry. Brush the starfish with a mixture of half glue and half water. Dust with white glitter. Let dry.

HERE'S HOW
to embellish the Pillar Candles
On protected surface lay pillar candle on its side between two heat resistant objects. Briefly (one to two seconds) heat one area of the candle with a heat gun. Immediately remove the heat and press one mirror rosette into the melted surface of the candle and remove. (This works well if you hold the rosette in one hand and the heat gun in the other hand.) Repeat this process on the entire surface of the candle until it is covered. Repeat this process on the other pillars.

HERE'S HOW
to make the Mirror Rosette Garland Embellishments
Measure and snip one piece of wire 3 feet long. Coil the first 3 inches of one end by wrapping the wire around a wood skewer. Thread one rosette onto the long end of wire. Thread the wire up through the center of the rosette. Then thread one crystal bead. Bend the wire and loop it back through the center of rosette out the back of rosette. Wrap wire seven times around skewer. Thread the next rosette and bead, coil wire again, etc. Continue until all six sets of rosettes and beads have been attached. Wrap around the base of pillar. Twist wire ends with needle nose pliers to secure. Cut off excess wire and tuck twisted wire behind one rosette. Place rosette garland around base of candle. Repeat process for the remaining two pillars.

Never leave a burning candle unattended.

Mirror Rosette Embellished White Pillars
Shown on page 119

WHAT YOU NEED
3-inch-diameter white pillar candles
2 solid heat-resistant objects
    (such as bricks)
Heat gun
19 mirror rosettes
Wire snips

26-gauge aluminum wire
Wood skewer (or a similar object
    to wrap wire around)
Long nose pliers
Ruler
6 mm faceted crystal beads such as
    Swarovski, 1 per rosette

3-D Fabric Snowflake Ornaments

Shown on page 118

WHAT YOU NEED

Tracing paper or copier
Pencil
Scissors
½ yard 44-inch-wide lightweight white
    cotton fabric (6 inches for each
    ornament)
½ yard heavy weight iron-on adhesive
Marking pencil
Pearly fabric paint
Matching sewing thread
Nylon thread

HERE'S HOW

1. Trace or copy desired patterns, *below* and on *pages 125 and 126*, and cut out. Set aside.

2. Iron adhesive onto the back side of one layer of white cotton fabric. Remove the paper backing and iron on another layer of white cotton fabric to sandwich the other, right sides out. Place the desired paper pattern and trace onto the stiffened white fabric, cutting out three of the same shapes for each snowflake. Carefully cut out shapes. With fabric paint add shapes and lines to decorate the snowflake shapes. After paint is dry, layer three snowflakes exactly on top of

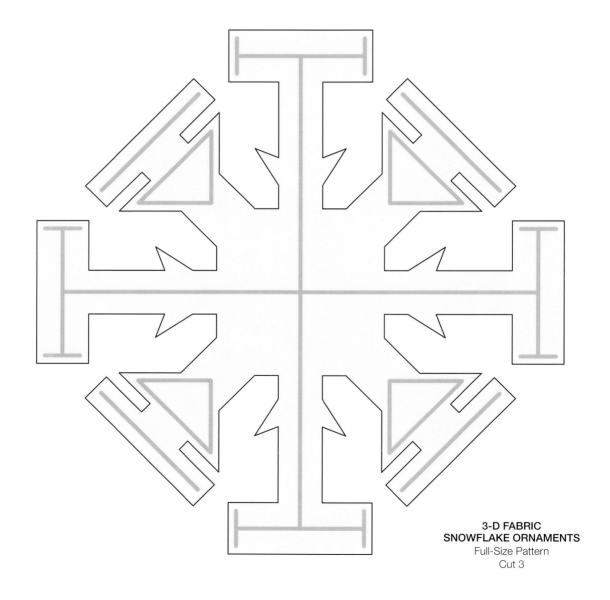

**3-D FABRIC
SNOWFLAKE ORNAMENTS**
Full-Size Pattern
Cut 3

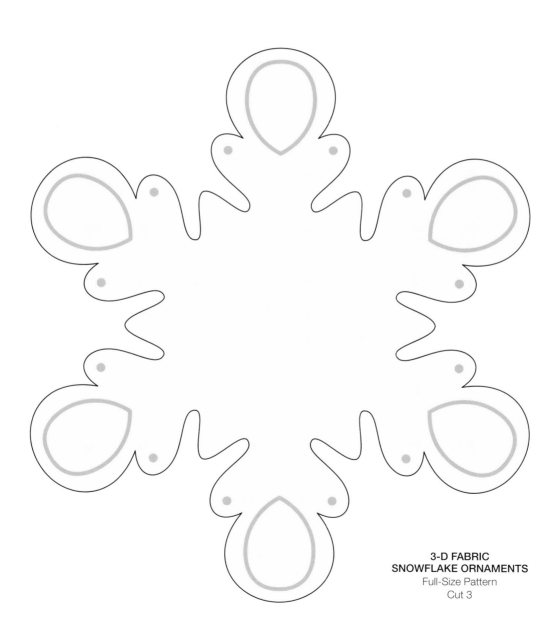

each other and machine-stitch together down the middle in a straight line. Open up and crease along the stitching line to fan out layers for a 3-D snowflake. With a needle and nylon thread, stitch through the top of the ornament to create a loop to hang the ornament.

**3-D FABRIC
SNOWFLAKE ORNAMENTS**
Full-Size Pattern
Cut 3

White Crystal Ornaments

Shown on page 120

WHAT YOU NEED

White matte-finish ornament
Clear glass hinged ornament
Chandelier crystal beads and teardrop
Silver jump rings
Crystal rhinestone stickers
Long nose pliers (two pair are best)
26-gauge aluminum wire
Wire snips
Strong crafts glue such as Quick Grip
   all-purpose permanent adhesive

**3-D FABRIC
SNOWFLAKE ORNAMENTS**
Full-Size Pattern
Cut 3

HERE'S HOW

to make the Matte-Finish Ornament

1. Insert a chandelier crystal bead connector between ornament cap and ornament hanger wire. Glue ornament cap to ornament. Let dry.

2. Insert large silver jump rings into the four outer holes of the chandelier connector. Attach a string of crystal beads (approximately four beads) to each large jump ring. Add a chandelier connector to the bottom of ornament using large jump rings and attach bottom ends of the four strands of crystal beads.

HERE'S HOW

to make the Clear Glass Hinged Ornament

1. Cut a piece of wire about 5 inches long. Thread it through the top of a chandelier bead/teardrop. Thread both ends of the wire up through the ornament cap so teardrop dangles inside hinged glass ornament. Wrap the wire ends around ornament hanger wire. Cut off excess wire.

2. Press crystal rhinestone stickers onto outside of glass ornament.

White Beaded Tree Topper
Shown on page 121

WHAT YOU NEED
7 white pearl sprigs
3-inch round, 2-inch deep plastic foam circle
Crafts glue
Scissors; fine wire

HERE'S HOW
Lay five sprigs of pearls around the circle to form a five-pointed star and stick them into the plastic foam. Secure with glue. Cut some of the pearls from the remaining two sprigs and glue to the front of the star. Allow to dry. Secure the wire to the back of the star by winding it around the stems to attach to the tree.

Bead and Rose Garland
Shown on page 121

WHAT YOU NEED
White roses
Scissors
Small bowl of water
White dental floss
Long sewing needle
Glass beads with holes to accommodate the needle

HERE'S HOW
Cut the tops from the roses, leaving about a ¼-inch stem, and place in the bowl of water. Cut a length of dental floss and thread the needle. Start by threading a bead on the floss. Tie the bead to the end. Thread the roses onto the needle at the rose base. Continue threading the beads and roses until the desired length of garland is completed.

make it
sparkle

*Give your holiday a little extra shimmer
and shine with all kinds of decorating projects
that sparkle with the season.*

Create a **Golden Feather Wreath,** *opposite,* with bright
pinecones and touches of sparkling glitter to hang in an
entryway or on a pretty door. Reflect upon the season
as you enjoy **Vintage Rhinestone Votives,** *above,* designed
to show off some of Grandma's jewelry. Instructions for
both projects are on *page 136.*

Let nature be the inspiration for a **Sparkling Hydrangea Banister,** *opposite*. Start by adding some shine to dried hydrangeas with orange glitter. Metallic birds and fresh orange slices complete the stunning arrangement. Simple-to-make **Curlicue Sparkle Ornaments,** *below left,* show off lime green glitter on a pretty orange ball. **Jeweled Trims,** *below right,* are created in minutes using stick-on square jewels. Instructions for all of the projects are on *pages 136–137.*

Make a pretty **Shimmering Snowflake Stocking,** *below,* by using fabric that has a natural shine. Add a satin or taffeta pin-tucked cuff to complete the stocking. Group sherbet glasses filled with shiny Christmas balls and greens to make a **Simply Elegant Centerpiece,** *opposite.* Instructions are on *pages 138–139.*

Holiday ornaments come together with extra pizzazz to create a **Pretty and Bright Wreath,** *opposite.* Choose the colors that fit your decorating scheme this season. Clear and sparkling **Rock Candy Tie-Ups,** *bottom left,* make a sweet table favor. Create lots of shimmer and shine with a simple **Pushpin Trim,** *above.* Instructions for all of these projects are on *page 139.*

Golden Feather Wreath

Shown on page 128

WHAT YOU NEED

6 pinecones
Small handsaw
Gold spray paint
Fir tree branches
Tacky glue
Gold glitter
Hot glue gun and hot glue sticks
Purchased feather wreath

HERE'S HOW

Bake pinecones for 20 minutes. Using the handsaw, remove the bottom end of the pinecones. On a protected surface spray paint the pinecones and fir branches gold (three coats, allowing drying time between coats of paint). Apply tacky glue to the tips of a pinecone and sprinkle with gold glitter. Gently shake pinecone to remove excess glitter. Let dry. Repeat procedure on remaining pinecones. Hot-glue pinecones and fir branches to feather wreath using a hot-glue gun.

Vintage Rhinestone Votives

Shown on page 129

WHAT YOU NEED

Assorted rhinestone earrings, pins, etc.
3 clear glass votive cups with flat sides
Metal snips
Metal file
Scissors
Sheer olive ribbon
Double-sided tape
Strong crafts glue such as Quick Grip
  all-purpose permanent adhesive

HERE'S HOW

1. Select desired rhinestone earrings, pins, etc. (Tip: Look for items that have fairly flat backs so they can be easily glued to the flat surface of the glass votives.) Using metal snips, cut off protruding pin backs, earring posts, or clips. Use a small metal file to smooth any rough edges left after removal.
2. Cut sheer ribbon slightly longer than the circumference of votive cup. Apply double-sided tape to ribbon end (top and bottom) and secure to one corner of the votive. Wrap ribbon around votive and secure ribbon with tape to each corner. Cut off excess ribbon. Repeat procedure with other votives.
3. Using strong adhesive, begin gluing rhinestone items to one side of each votive at a time. Let dry thoroughly before continuing. Insert colorful votive candles when project is finished. To clean, gently wipe with cloth; do not wash votive cups.

Never leave a burning candle unattended.

Curlicue Sparkle Ornaments

Shown on page 130

WHAT YOU NEED

Purchased matte-finish ornaments
  in desired colors
Drinking glass tumbler
Crafts glue with fine tip
Lime green fine glitter

HERE'S HOW

Place an ornament in the tumbler to secure it while working. Starting at the top of the ball, make swirls or curlicues with the glue. Dust with glitter. Allow to dry.

Jeweled Trims
Shown on page 130

WHAT YOU NEED
Purchased ornaments in desired colors
Purchased square jewel stickers
    (available at crafts and scrapbook
    stores)

HERE'S HOW
Remove the stickers from the package
and place on an ornament leaving equal
spaces between. Continue placing stickers
on the ball until a polka-dot effect is
achieved.

Sparkling Hydrangea Banister
Shown on page 131

WHAT YOU NEED
Fresh or artificial greenery garland
24-gauge wire; wire cutters
Spray bottle; water
Crafts glue
Dried hydrangeas
Orange glitter
Purchased bird ornaments
Fine copper or brass wire
Fresh orange slices
2-inch-wide sheer orange ribbon

HERE'S HOW
Arrange the greenery on the banister
and wire in place. Fill the spray bottle
with a mixture of half glue and half water.
Set aside. On a protected surface lay the
hydrangeas out separately and spray
lightly with the mixture. Immediately
dust with the orange glitter. Allow to dry.
Wire to the greenery. Clip or use fine
wire to attach the birds to the greenery.
Wire the orange slices to the greenery
and run an orange bow through the
length of the arrangement. Tie a bow
at the newel post.

3. With right sides together, sew short side of cuff piece to form a circular tube and do the same for the cuff lining. With right sides together, sew bottom edges of cuff and cuff lining. Turn right side out and press lower edge. Place hanging loop down inside stocking at side edge; overlap raw edges of ends at top edge of stocking and baste in place.

Insert the cuff inside the stocking with the right side of the cuff against the wrong side of the stocking, keeping top raw edges even. Sew around the top edge through all layers using a ⅜-inch seam allowance.

4. Flip cuff piece out over front of stocking and press top seam flat. Apply snowflake embellishments to cuff front.

Shimmering Snowflake Stocking

Shown on page 132

WHAT YOU NEED

Tracing paper or copier; scissors
¼ yard cotton snowflake print fabric
¼ yard coordinating fabric for cuff
Double needle for sewing machine
Snowflake embellishments (stickers
   from scrapbook store)
Coordinating color embroidery floss;
   needle; matching thread

HERE'S HOW

1. Enlarge and copy the patterns onto tracing paper. Place right sides of snowflake print fabric together and cut two of the stocking patterns and a 2×7-inch-strip for the hanging loop.

2. Before cutting the cuff piece, sew pin-tucking to a section for the cuff. Using a double needle in the sewing machine, sew straight lines across fabric. Note that pin-tucking shrinks the fabric, so allow extra fabric to cut the cuff pattern. Cut one cuff pattern from the pin-tucked fabric and one from untucked cuff fabric for the cuff lining. Mark stitching lines on toe and heel sections. Stitch lines using running stitch, *page 160.* With right sides together stitch around side and lower edges of the stocking pieces, leaving top edges open, using a ¼-inch seam allowance. Clip curves; turn right side out and press lightly. With right sides together sew long edge of loop piece together. Turn right side out and press.

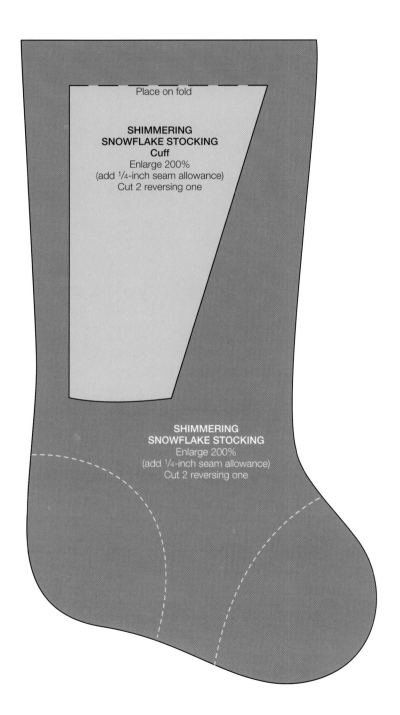

Place on fold

**SHIMMERING
SNOWFLAKE STOCKING
Cuff**
Enlarge 200%
(add ¼-inch seam allowance)
Cut 2 reversing one

**SHIMMERING
SNOWFLAKE STOCKING**
Enlarge 200%
(add ¼-inch seam allowance)
Cut 2 reversing one

Simply Elegant Centerpiece
Shown on page 133

WHAT YOU NEED
Clear glass sherbet goblets
Small ornaments in desired colors
Long, spiral ornaments
Fresh evergreens
Small silver beaded sprays

HERE'S HOW
Be sure that the goblets are clean and dry. Arrange them in a row on the table. Fill with ornaments, greens, and sprays. Lay additional long, spiral ornaments on the table between the goblets.

Pretty and Bright Wreath
Shown on page 134

WHAT YOU NEED
12-inch-diameter plastic foam wreath
White or pale blue ribbon
Hot glue gun and glue sticks
Christmas tree ornaments in various sizes, sheens, and textures in desired colors

HERE'S HOW
Wrap the foam wreath with white or pale blue ribbon. Secure with hot glue. Hot-glue the variety of glass tree ornaments onto it and onto each other; be sure to use an assortment of colors, textures, and sheens for the most interesting effect. Allow to dry.

Pushpin Trim
Shown on page 135

WHAT YOU NEED
3-inch plastic foam ball
Dozens of clear push pins
Silver chenille stem

HERE'S HOW
Starting at the center of the ball, insert the clear pushpins around the center of the ball. Continue to add rows to cover the ball. Bend the chenille stem and insert into the top for a hanger.

Rock Candy Tie-Ups
Shown on page 135

WHAT YOU NEED
3 sticks of clear rock candy
Colored cording

HERE'S HOW
Overlap the rock candy and tie with a piece of colored cording. Lay in the center of a plate.

scrapbooking paper holiday

*Have fun making all kinds of paper
crafts as well as easy scrapbook layouts
using the holiday papers available to every
lucky crafter at Christmastime.*

Send a handmade greeting by making your own **Purple
Snowflake Card,** *opposite.* The snowflakes are pretty
stickers added to purple card stock. A **Red Ornament
Greeting,** *above,* is pretty enough to display. The round
paper ornament shapes bring a whole new level to paper
fun. Instructions for both projects are on *page 150.*

Sure to become an annual tradition, this stunning **Paper Advent Box**, *opposite and above,* makes use of a variety of scrapbook papers and a wooden shadow box. Each little door hides a sweet surprise. Instructions for making this clever box are on *page 150.*

Make some **Paper Treat Trays**, *opposite,* using printed scrapbook paper—then add goodies in a waffle cup dish to set on top. Hide a candy coin under the cups for fun. **Money Bags,** *right,* will be a welcome gift on the tree. The pockets that hold the money are made from scrapbook papers in shapes that you choose. Instructions and a variety of patterns for both projects are on *pages 151–153.*

Make a charming **Stationery Set and Matching Paper Clips,** *above,* using rubber stamps, attractive papers, and shrink art. Instructions for making this set are on *page 151.* Create your own **Simple Scrapbook Layouts,** *opposite and pages 148–149,* using just three simple steps—color, design, embellish. Turn the page for more layouts.

Handmade Holiday

You've always enjoyed making Christmas presents for family. Everyone loved the special scrapbooks you made this year!

Make dozens of **Simple Scrapbook Layouts,** *page 147, right and opposite,* using the same basic concept of choosing color, design, and embellishments that fit your photos. Instructions, tips, and sources for making the pages are on *pages 154–158.*